HARSH GRIEF,
GENTLE HOPE

HARSH GRIEF GENTLE HOPE

MARY A. WHITE

NAVPRESS

BRINGING TRUTH TO LIFE

NavPress Publishing Group

P.O. Box 35001, Colorado Springs, Colorado 80935

The Navigators is an international Christian organization. Jesus Christ gave His followers the Great Commission to go and make disciples (Matthew 28:19). The aim of The Navigators is to help fulfill that commission by multiplying laborers for Christ in every nation.

NavPress is the publishing ministry of The Navigators. NavPress publications are tools to help Christians grow. Although publications alone cannot make disciples or change lives, they can help believers learn biblical discipleship, and apply what they learn to their lives and ministries.

Library of Congress Catalog Card Number: 95-7657
ISBN 08910-99085

Cover photographs: The Stock Solution and Westlight

Some of the people and events in this book are true to life and are included with the permission of the persons involved.

Unless otherwise identified, all Scripture quotations in this publication are taken from the *HOLY BIBLE: NEW INTERNATIONAL VERSION®* (NIV®). Copyright © 1973, 1978, 1984 by International Bible Society. Used by permission of Zondervan Publishing House. All rights reserved.

White, Mary, 1935-
    Harsh grief, gentle hope / by Mary A. White
       p. cm.
    ISBN 0-89109-908-5
    1. Bereavement—Religious aspects—Christianity.
2. Grief—Religious aspects—Christianity. 3. Children—Death—Religious aspects—Christianity. 4. Consolation.
5. White, Mary, 1935-
I. Title.
BV4907.W565   1995
248.8'6—dc20   95-7657
                                      CIP

Printed in the United States of America

1 2 3 4 5 6 7 8 9 10/99 98 97 96 95

FOR A FREE CATALOG OF
NAVPRESS BOOKS & BIBLE STUDIES,
CALL 1-800-366-7788 (USA)
or 1-416-499-4615 (CANADA)

Contents

Preface

There is not a word in the English language to describe the loss of a child. *Widow* describes the loss of a spouse; *orphan* defines loss of mother and father; but when bereaved parents need to tell of their suffering, no single word carries the painful message. Instead, parents have to state the achingly sad fact every time.

"My son died."

"My daughter was killed."

"Someone murdered my child."

There is a subtle shift of emphasis between the words, "I'm a widow," and "My son died." Small, but painful. The emphasis for bereaved parents remains on the sad past rather than the painful present with possible hopes for the future.

The lack of a word to define the sorrow parents feel when their child dies illustrates their expectations for the future, which died with their child. All of the plans, dreams, love, effort, and anticipation that a parent puts into a child's future crumbles when he dies. Reality takes on a bleak loneliness only dimly imagined by those who haven't suffered the loss.

The fact that our culture has abandoned the trappings of grief—the visual cues—only increases the sense of loss. Black clothing now signifies an elegant evening out, not mourning. Dark armbands never appear after a death. Black crepe above the door hasn't been seen in decades. Bereavement is shunned, as are the bereaved, by society as a whole.

Perhaps because we live in such an unstable and violent society, we turn away from the daily threat of death. If someone mourns, we hope they will do so privately and not intrude on our emotional space. We falsely imagine that because they look and function *normally*, grief isn't taking a toll.

Those who would like to extend grace and comfort have no visible sign to indicate how long a person is grieving, and there is no outward indication to determine if a new acquaintance we meet has suffered a severe, recent loss.

We can't change the habits and dictates of our society; they are deeply embedded in our cultural fabric. But we can all be more sensitized to the grief and loss those around us bear.

All loss hurts. Lingering loss due to extended illness brings added pain to those who watch the beloved one suffer. Sudden loss due to accident, trauma, or homicide impacts loved ones with shock, sorrow, and regret, for they were denied a chance to say goodbye. There was no final hug, kiss, kind word, or happy moment.

One purpose of this book is to describe some of the shock, horror, and overwhelming sorrow I felt when our beloved and only son died in a homicide. An assassin wiped out his life with the quick pull of a trigger. No explanation, no reason exists that can rationalize the taking of his life. His murder brought immediate, agonizing pain to his family and friends.

Murder defies the laws of God and outrages the sensitivities of decent people. The murder rate in the United States is climbing so dramatically that the impact on personal lives has become lost in the statistics. The suffering in the aftermath of a murder takes an unbelievable toll on our *entire* society when we lose the lifetime potential of those murdered. The numbing, stifling effect on loved ones left behind also takes a drastic toll.

In spite of our agonizing grief, we did learn to go on after Steve's homicide. My healing proceeded one little step at a time. Eventually, acceptance came, along with a measure of peace. Not acceptance of murder, for that is impossible, but acceptance of my terrible loss and Steve's absence.

Beyond the pain and grief came quiet, gentle hope from God. Slowly, very slowly, the shock, horror, and sorrow receded, and healing began. I hope that in telling the story of Steve's murder and my sorrow, other grieving families will find some understanding of their grief, and with it a degree of hope and peace.

Chapter 1

"PLEASE DON'T LET IT BE TRUE"

Our son was senselessly and brutally murdered on a cool, clear evening late in April 1990. Those are the cold facts, a condensation of the police report. There is no way to soften the story. He died. He was the innocent victim of a random homicide. A statistic. But the facts don't convey the devastation to his family and friends from losing him.

Steve drove a cab in our growing but still moderately sized town of Colorado Springs. He also conducted his own radio show on the local public radio station. He dreamed of breaking into radio full time. He wanted to develop specific and unique music and talk shows. In the meantime, he drove a taxi to meet expenses. He was murdered in that cab.

Jerry and I were traveling the day Steve died. Our trip included a few days in Canada visiting with Navigator staff friends there. Then we stopped in Columbus, Ohio, to present a seminar at a large music conference that also included life-values seminars and Bible teaching.

We arrived on Thursday in time to attend an evening concert presented by well-known Christian music artists. Beautiful, expressive music flowed over us during the evening. Some of the music was stimulating, some soothing, some meditative.

The next morning, as we prepared to leave our hotel room to meet friends before presenting our seminar, the phone rang.

Jerry answered it and said, "Hi, Marjie."

It was common to hear from Jerry's secretary, Marjie, who kept close touch with us on our trips.

I glanced at Jerry as he answered and saw the blood drain from his face. His features literally collapsed. I watched his respiration deepen and accelerate. He dropped onto the side of the bed. I knew something terrible had happened.

He said, "When?" Then listened.

He turned to me, drew me into the shelter of his arm, and said, "Steve was murdered last night. The police need to know who his dentist was for identification." Then he turned back to the phone.

I felt my heart shatter and break. I wrapped my arms around my rib cage to hold myself together. I couldn't breathe. The edges of my vision darkened and my mind went numb. Aloud I whispered, "Oh God, oh God, oh God, oh God. . . . Please, no, no."

It can't be true. There must be some mistake. I must still be sleeping. I'll wake up now. Oh dear God, please. Please. Please don't let it be true. Let it be a dream.

As Jerry continued to talk with Marjie, making arrangements to return home immediately, I paced the room. Occasionally I sat down beside Jerry, but then I would leap up again to renew my aimless pacing as I listened to the ever-worsening, one-sided conversation. I was drawn again and again to the window to stare at the bleakness outside.

On this late April day, the trees in the empty fields outside the hotel were still bare, their stark branches pointing skyward, blown by a spring wind. Brown grass covered the ground. Gray clouds scuttled low overhead. That colorless world mirrored the desolation that swept through my soul.

I began throwing things aimlessly into our suitcases. Jerry finished his phone call with Marjie and turned to me. We fell into each other's arms and began sobbing.

"Jerry, it can't be true. Isn't there some mistake? Please tell me it's not true."

13

Oh, God. I can't believe this. It can't be true. Our dear Steve, murdered? Who? Why? This can't be happening. Please, God, don't let it be true.

Jerry gently put me aside to call the county sheriff's department. When he finished, we sat on the bed with our arms around one another, weeping, while he told me what little the detectives knew about the murder.

Steve's body had been discovered in the front seat of his cab around 11:30 p.m. the night before. A passing policeman had stopped to investigate and was appalled by the grisly scene that greeted him. He was shocked to see bullet holes in the windshield. The investigation was underway, and homicide detectives would give us more information as the day progressed.

Jerry called the conference office to tell them Steve had been murdered. We were leaving immediately for home and wouldn't be able to conduct our seminar. Immediately—one thousand strong—the conference attendees prayed for us. With that act, a stream of kindness and caring and sympathy and prayer began to flow toward us that continues even now.

A MAD DASH TO THE AIRPORT

Our friends had not yet arrived at the hotel. The hotel manager, hearing our story, offered us a ride to the airport. He told us we wouldn't have enough time to wait for a taxi and still make the flight connection that Marjie had arranged for us. He used his own car, a small all terrain vehicle with open sides and back. We crammed in.

As we raced along the freeway with the wind whipping our clothes and hair, conversation was mercifully impossible. I felt like I was living in a nightmare. I wanted to wake up. I hoped I would wake up. I *prayed* to wake up. A strong sense of disbelief, of unreality, swept over me.

When we arrived at the airport, we ran for the gate, calling back our thanks to the hotel manager for his kindness. The door to the jetway was already closed. The United Airlines supervisor who accompanied us from the check-in counter told the gate agent to open it.

"But we're closed," he protested.

"Open it," the supervisor commanded. A significant kindness by a huge, impersonal company. We dropped into seats near the rear of the plane that would take us to Chicago for a connecting flight to Denver and home.

As soon as the seat-belt sign flashed off, Jerry went to the back of the plane to call Julie, Steve's wife. She was in shock, distraught and reeling from her early morning encounter with the police who had come to notify her of Steve's murder.

The man sitting next to me began to converse. He complained at length about the unpredictable and unpleasant Chicago weather.

How bizarre that this man complains about the weather as though it were a major problem. Doesn't he know, can't he sense, that I'm dying inside? My only son is dead. At least he is alive to observe the weather, good or bad. How trivial, how very small a problem to face bad weather.

I couldn't respond. Unbidden and unchecked, the tears streamed down my face. Perhaps our seatmate finally noticed, for he suddenly became engrossed in reading the flight magazine. At one point the thought crossed my mind that this would be a fine opportunity to speak of the grace of God in a calamity, but I couldn't trust my voice enough to speak.

Please, God, this can't be true. I can't believe it. Our Steve, murdered? Our dear Steve, dead?

BREAKING THE NEWS TO FAMILY

In the Chicago airport, we called Dave, our daughter Kathy's husband, and Tim, our daughter Karen's husband, asking them to go home from work and be with Kathy and Karen as we called to tell them of Steve's murder. We knew the local media would report the killing on the midday news in Colorado Springs, and we couldn't bear for Kathy to hear of her brother's death on the radio or TV. Karen, in Seattle, would need Tim's presence to help her face the horrifying, unthinkable news.

We called on adjoining phones, turning our backs to other hurrying travelers as we tried to hide our tears and stifled sobs. It broke my heart anew to hear my daughters' stricken reaction to the news of their brother's death. Stunned and grieving, the presence and comfort of their husbands helped them cope with the initial shock.

We also called my sister Marty in Colorado Springs, knowing she, too, would likely hear the news on public media. She received the news calmly enough as we spoke with her, but when she tried to notify our brother Dave and his wife, Rosalie, in Seattle, the shock hit her and she sobbed so violently she couldn't relate the account of Steve's death for several minutes.

As we hurried to the next flight, tormenting thoughts returned.

God, can it really be true? How could it happen? Steve was so quick-witted, so careful; surely there must be some mistake. Please, Lord, let there be a mistake; maybe it was somebody else. Maybe Steve loaned out his cab. No. No, then some other mother would be feeling this wrenching grief that I'm feeling. I don't want that, God. Just, please, please help us through this terrible thing.

As we boarded the flight to Denver, we were invited to sit in the back row of the first-class section where we would have a measure of privacy. Apparently, someone had placed a note beside our name in the airline computer regarding the murder.

A kind flight attendant told us, "I'm so sorry for your loss." My tears began to flow again with her expression of concern for us, strangers to her.

I made a valiant effort to curb my tears when someone might be watching me. The attempt was futile. Someone later told us that in times of grief, we don't choose our emotions, they choose us. We had no way to predict or control or stop the tears.

Shortly after take-off, the flight attendants served lunch. Jerry urged me to eat, but I could not force food past the growing lump in my throat. I felt drained, desperately tired, but I couldn't rest. I did have a voracious thirst and drank copious amounts of water and juice. Jerry held me, and for much of the trip we sat silently clinging to one another, occasionally sighing, "I can't believe it."

Fragments of Scripture raced through my mind. *"When you pass through the waters, I will be with you. . . . Those who hope in the Lord will renew their* strength. . . . *The Lord is close to the brokenhearted. . . ."*

God, help us, please. I don't know if I can bear this. How can Jerry bear it? His only son is dead. Is our dear Steve really gone? Can it really be true?

Oh God, I accept this terrible news. But help me, help me. Give me strength.

Chapter 2

THE NEWS SPREADS

W hen we reached Denver, we rented a car and drove to meet our youngest daughter, Kristie. As we passed through the familiar Colorado countryside, aimless thoughts floated through my mind. Although Jerry had accepted the news as accurate, I could not still the hollow hope that maybe there had been a mistake.

Didn't the police ask for Steve's dentist's name to verify the victim by the dental records? Could it be they didn't know for sure? Could someone else have used the cab? Maybe the wound was so terrible the police couldn't identify who it was. Maybe, just maybe. . . .

Kristie was in her third year at Colorado State University in Fort Collins. From the Chicago airport we had asked Kathy to call Kristie and let her know we would be stopping by later in the day to see her. But we asked Kathy not to tell Kristie of her brother's death. To hear the news alone, over the telephone, would crush her.

Kathy's phone call to Kristie gave her no inkling of the disaster that had taken place, and it spared Kristie the ordeal of hearing the news alone, without family support. Kathy expressed great strength as she made that phone call without giving a hint of the grief she was feeling.

Friendly and upbeat by nature, Kristie greeted us with her usual, "Hi, Dad. Hi, Mom. What's up?"

We hugged her and said, "Why don't we sit in the car? We have something we want to talk to you about."

Kristie asked, "What? What? Did I mess up my finances?" Always a concern for a college student!

We sat on either side of her in the back seat of the car. Gently, Jerry said, "We have some bad news. Steve was killed last night."

Her face blanched, much as Jerry's had earlier in the day. Then, on a long keening scream, she cried, "Who murdered my brother? Who killed my brother?" Her uncontrollable weeping continued for many minutes. We folded her in our arms and wept with her.

Her immediate assumption that Steve had been murdered startled me. From the way Jerry presented the news, it could have been a traffic accident or any other type of accidental death. Later, when we asked her about that response, she didn't remember asking the question.

Kristie sensed a special bond with Steve. They looked alike, they often thought alike, and they enjoyed many of the same things. They treasured a special friendship. Perhaps, intuitively she presumed the worst possible death when she heard he was gone.

We all knew there was an element of risk in cab driving, even in Colorado Springs. Several times Steve told us of menacing situations he had encountered, but he seemed to have an intuitive feel for danger and avoided suspicious customers and risky locations.

In anticipation of possible trouble, he often carried a stout board under the front seat of his cab. He never hesitated to bypass a customer if the circumstances seemed at all threatening. His persistent caution made his murder all the more unthinkable.

Finally, Kristie calmed enough to go to her roommate and tell her what had happened. She sobbed violently as she related the news, sagging as Michelle and I held her in our arms, wailing her grief and disbelief.

Without bothering to pack, Kristie climbed into the car with us, and we drove the two hours home. Kristie and I sat in the back seat with our arms around one another while Jerry drove.

We alternated between reading several passages in the Bible, praying, crying, and riding in stunned silence. From time to time one of us would sigh, "I can't believe this is true," as tears slid down our cheeks. We repeated that mournful litany again and again in the coming days.

A tragedy, so unexpected and horrifying, takes time to absorb. Disbelief is a merciful, if momentary, respite.

THE ARMS OF FAMILY AND FRIENDS

We arrived home at dusk to find friends and family waiting to receive us with warm embraces and kind words. As many people took us in their arms, most could only whisper our names or choke "I'm so sorry" before lapsing into sympathetic silence. Their tears streamed with ours as together we faced the unthinkable.

Marty was there, her face drawn and sad. Our friendship went beyond the bonds of family. We truly enjoyed being together—talking, laughing. Our children were close friends. Over the years we had often taken care of one another's children. Losing Steve was almost as painful to her as losing one of her own.

Longtime Navigator friends and coworkers were waiting to extend their care and love and help—dear colleagues who had known us for years, now struck numb as we were by the magnitude of our loss.

Ken, a warm, empathetic friend from church spoke for our church family when he expressed his grief with tears and hugs.

Dave and Kathy were waiting at the house to embrace us. We wept in each other's arms.

Kathy whispered to me, "Oh, Mom, I feel so bad for you; but God will help us."

She voiced our overriding thought during those first days after Steve's murder: Only God could truly help us through the shock, the sorrow, the over-whelming sense of loss, the complete bewilderment that follows any murder.

Beautiful flower bouquets had arrived during the day. Friends had brought food, cleaned the house, made endless calls to friends, family, and staff. We had very few answers regarding the murder, but someone stayed by the phone accepting the continuous stream of phone calls from those who cared and from the merely curious. Someone called our doctor to order sleeping pills.

Marjie had spent the day calling and faxing Navigator staff around the world. Phone messages and return faxes awaited us, assuring us of the prayers, sympathy, and comfort of dear colleagues. Jerry also maintained a presence in the Air Force Reserves, and many of them had called to send their sympathy and offers of help. The kindness and caring overwhelmed us and caused more tears to flow.

Someone gave us the message that the identification of Steve's body had been completed. That crushed the final bit of hope I had harbored. Steve was dead. Murdered. Gone.

Father God, I still can't believe it, even though they tell me it's true. Help me, please. Help our family. Bless these dear friends surrounding us with love and care. Welcome our dear Steve to Heaven. Please tell him I love him. Tell him I'm sorry, so very sorry. Tell him I'll miss him so much.

Steve's wife, Julie, arrived—stunned, grieving,

feeling helpless, as we all were. It had been a truly terrible day for her, starting with the early morning arrival of the police to notify her of Steve's murder. She had been preparing to leave for the elementary school where she taught fourth grade. Alone, she faced the horrifying news and extended questioning by the police as they sought her help for some possible clue to the murder.

Frantic and grieving, she called family and friends, but found no one at home. Her brother had planned to meet Steve for a round of golf that morning and was already on the golf course. Her parents lived in the Washington, D.C. area. Her teaching colleagues were already at work.

In desperation she called Marjie, asking how to find us. At last she reached a friend who spent the day with her.

We held her and sobbed together. We urged her to spend the night with us, but she felt she had to start sleeping at home sometime and decided to confront the daunting challenge immediately. Embracing her a final time, we watched her leave, feeling a deep sorrow for her.

Near midnight, Karen and Tim and baby Jerad arrived with our dear friend Alice Canlis. At the time, Tim was the associate pastor of a church in Seattle. As soon as Jerry and I drew them into our embrace the tears flowed again. They were in shock, as we were, and only the falling tears could release some of the impact of the horrible news.

One final, difficult task remained for that long, long day. We placed a call to my sister Ruth, a missionary in Kenya. It was early Saturday morning there. One of our Navigator staff leaders had arrived at her home shortly before our phone call to tell her of Steve's death.

Even as we called she was packing to come home. All that day, friends helped her pack, close her apartment, arrange airline tickets, and get to the airport. Flight reservations are often difficult to book in Kenya due to heavy tourist and business travel. Miraculously, Ruth was able to board a flight that night.

Through that long flight home (it takes nearly thirty hours), she traveled alone with her thoughts and grief and tears. She, too, had cared for Steve in his childhood, watched him grow to manhood, lived at intervals in our home, and she deeply mourned his death. On that prolonged flight, several people noticed her distress, and listened and helped.

THE SLEEPLESS NIGHTS BEGIN

Sometime after midnight everyone settled for the night, some with nearby friends, and our family in our home. Jerry and I wearily made our way to our bedroom. Although exhaustion overwhelmed us, sleep seemed impossible. With our arms around one another, we dropped to our knees beside our bed.

With sobs breaking his voice, Jerry prayed and placed our son back into the arms of God much as we had received him as a gift from God thirty years before. Jerry told God we accepted Steve's death and we received from God whatever He chose for us. With that prayerful release of our precious son, we wept together for a long time.

Jerry and I felt the need of sleeping pills that first night. In spite of the sedative effect, we awakened several times, jerked from drugged sleep into the shocking

25

reality of Steve's murder. I awakened to physical pain in my stomach and a horrible shuddering that rippled over my entire body as the dreadful memory raced through my mind.

Murder? Murder!? Shot three times in the head? Steve's brain destroyed? Steve's mind that registered a genius IQ? That reasoned, laughed, joked, dreamed? Was his face blown away? How can it be? How could anyone shoot another person in the head? Why? Why? Did Steve see it coming? Was he threatened? Did he plead for his life? Was he tortured? Did he try to save himself? Did he call for me? Or Julie? Or his father? Or You?

Did he die right away? Did he suffer? Oh, God, I should have been there. I'm his mother. He shouldn't have died alone like that, helpless, murdered, entombed in his cab. It's not fair. It's not fair. Please, God, I can't bear this. . . . Help me to think of something else.

"Do not fear, for I am with you. . . . Do not be dismayed. . . . I am your God. . . . I will strengthen you and help you. . . . I am always with you."

And then the blessed, numbing blackness of sleep again for a short while.

Chapter 3

COPING WITH THE DETAILS OF DEATH

Morning finally came, bringing an intensifying horror and grief as we faced all that a homicide means to a family. Murder causes unimaginable complications. We faced the paralyzing shock of Steve's untimely and brutal death, endless consultations with the police, appalled reactions by friends, messages from the district attorney's office, newspaper interviews, television reports, court hearings—sorrow upon sorrow upon sorrow.

Murder destroys the loved one and continues to rip and tear and bruise the emotions and spirits of those left behind. Sometimes the wounds are never laid to rest, for the murderer goes uncaught and unpunished for the monstrous crime. We were just entering that forboding territory.

That first morning we knew only a small portion of what lay in store for us. Friends and family gathered at our home early in the morning. Weary, sad, and disbelieving, we tried to comfort one another.

About a dozen of us crowded around the dining room table with several others standing nearby holding their plates. Sipping orange juice and using my fork to push at the food on my plate, I listened to the conversations around me.

Someone had spoken with the sheriff's department that morning and they still had no clues regarding the killer.

"Maybe it was somebody on drugs."

"Could have been a drug deal that Steve witnessed."

"Maybe somebody tried to rob him, got scared, and ran off."

"The autopsy will let us know more about his murder."

Autopsy? Autopsy? Oh, dear God, they'll do an autopsy on Steve? Is that where he is right now? In a morgue? No, I know he is in Heaven, but his body is still here. Why does he have to have an autopsy? What a horrible invasion of his body.

Isn't it bad enough that he was murdered? That his head was destroyed? Does he have to be subjected to an autopsy? Oh, of course; it was a homicide. The law says there must be an autopsy. How terrible. How awful. I can't bear it. Oh, God, please. I must think of something else. Hurry. Hurry. Think of something else.

An image came of our anticipation and excitement as the day of Steve's birth drew near. We were so joyous in those long ago days. Would it be a boy who looked like Jerry? Or a little girl, petite and quiet like Jerry's mother and mine?

Jerry's grandmother came to help us during that time. Her pride in her first great-grandchild was boundless. After his birth, she spent hours watching him through the hospital nursery window, exclaiming, "I can't wait to get my hands on that sweet baby."

Her loving, gentle example as she taught me to care for him set a pattern I wanted to follow even when she returned home. The thought of that cherished baby, now a dead man, murdered, lying in the county morgue tormented me.

Overwhelmed, I dropped my head to the table and sobbed. Aloud I prayed, "Oh, Lord, help us all. This is so hard. So hard."

Ken, sitting next to me, gathered me close and let me weep. When I finally looked up again I realized that everyone at the table was weeping with me.

Slowly we wiped our eyes, and gradually, haltingly, the conversation resumed.

WHY WAS HE MURDERED?

Reporters from the local newspaper arrived to interview us. I couldn't find the emotional strength to speak with them, but Jerry did. At the time of the interviews, since we had no idea who had murdered Steve, we appreciated the willingness of the media to limit information about our family, especially our home location.

Sheriff's detectives arrived to give us further details of the murder and to question us about Steve's personal habits, hoping to discover a clue that might aid in finding the murderer.

They had closely questioned Julie as well, seeking any small clue that might help the investigation.

Julie told them, "I don't think you can find the killer. It could be anyone, and he could be far away by now."

They reluctantly conceded that possibility, for the clues were few. When they came to talk with us, they didn't emphasize that grim probability. They were kind and gentle with us then and throughout the long months that followed.

One speculation was that Steve had witnessed some illegal activity or had somehow intruded into an ominous situation. But, again, there was no evidence of that.

Robbery did not seem to be a motive, since Steve's wallet was untouched and his cab wasn't stolen. The police questioned if a vendetta against our family prompted the murder, although that conjecture seemed highly unlikely.

I felt no fear for my own safety, but I was desperately concerned about my family—our daughters, Julie, our cherished grandchildren. I felt keenly a need to protect and guard our remaining family members. Jerry, too, feared a risk for our family, and until a suspect was apprehended, he kept in close touch with the detectives investigating the murder.

The detectives related no details of Steve's death except to tell us that he died instantaneously.

Oh, God, I hope so. But did he see it coming? Did he know he was going to die? Did he know what was happening? Did he suffer? I can't bear to think that he suffered. Was he afraid?

Rest periods took on a bizarre form. I was very fatigued, but whenever I tried to relax, my mind would begin racing with painful thoughts. It took major effort to keep from dwelling on the devastating speculation of Steve's last minutes of life, the need for an autopsy, his body in the mortuary. Aching tremors would chase through my body, and if I did doze off I would awaken with tormenting pangs in my stomach as the realization of Steve's murder returned.

On Saturday afternoon, at Jerry's insistence, I was trying to rest when Julie arrived, weeping piteously. She had spent a few hours in her classroom preparing the lesson plans for the next week's substitute teacher.

An unexpected spring snowstorm had descended on Colorado Springs, leaving several inches of snow blanketing the newly green lawns. On her way home from the school, Julie drove past the area where the police officer found Steve's cab.

Steve's body had been found in a predominantly Catholic neighborhood. Someone in the community had placed a small wooden cross in the snow and laid fresh flowers beside it as a memorial to the slain taxi driver. The touching scene intensified the reality of Steve's murder. In an agony of grief and horror Julie came to tell us what she had seen.

Her sorrow was so palpable, so stark, that it renewed my own anguish for her. Never had I imagined a grief so deep, so penetrating, that it drove everything else into the background.

My heart broke for Julie, now a young widow, overwhelmed by such crushing grief. She faced a confusing maze of decisions and pressures in those early days following the murder. She is a woman of strength and fortitude, but nothing prepares a woman to lose her husband to murder. We could only hold her and love her as she entered the bewildering, painful, frightening days of early widowhood.

DECISIONS THAT COULDN'T WAIT

Later that day, Jerry, Kathy and I drove through the slush to the funeral home to discuss details of the burial arrangements and to select a casket. We met Julie and her parents there.

Sudden death plunged our family into immediate, debilitating, terrible mourning, leaving us weak and stunned. At the same time we were required to make major decisions about which we had given no thought and for which we had no preparation. Julie faced many such decisions in the few days before the funeral.

What a strange feeling to be dispassionately discussing business details and burial arrangements when my heart was breaking and all I wanted to do was scream out my grief and disbelief. I'm sure all of us in that room felt the same. But civilized restraints kept us from wailing our sadness.

A melancholy atmosphere pervades a mortuary. I noticed it when our parents died and we made arrangements for their memorial services. But with Steve's death, my reaction was intensified. I couldn't escape the feeling that it was unreal—that I would wake up soon and all the pain and anguish would vanish. The trip to the mortuary compelled me to face anew the finality of Steve's death.

The employees treated us courteously and deferentially, but the solemn quiet and the sad errand that brought us to the funeral home renewed my sorrow. I felt a deep grief in helping to choose a casket for my son's body still lying in the county morgue, awaiting the final autopsy results. I wanted to escape that mortuary with its quiet, somber atmosphere, dim lighting, and thick carpets that muffled all sound, even the sound of weeping.

Eventually we were back in the cold, heavy air again, making our way to the cemetery on ice-slickened streets. Friends loaned us their custom van so that several members of the family could ride together. Nearness to loved ones helped to ease the pain of several sad errands—to the funeral home, the floral shop, the cemetery. Between each errand or decision we needed closeness, not even communication, just the reassuring presence of those who loved Steve and mourned with us.

Julie knew of the oldest cemetery in the city not far from the home where she and Steve lived. Jerry and I had never seen it and had never attended a funeral there. She felt it would be a fitting place for

Steve's grave. When we arrived to select a gravesite, we understood her suggestion.

Tucked in a little valley on the far west side of the city, away from the bustle of traffic, it held a breath-taking view of the mountains. A narrow footpath led away from the cemetery into the rugged hills. Julie said Steve had often hiked that trail and others nearby. We chose a site on a gently sloping hillside under an aged elm tree. Even with a dismal gray sky overhead and snow covering the ground, the scene was magnificent.

This sad place is so beautiful. If only Steve could hike here once more. If only I could see him striding through these rugged hills, his dogs running alongside. If only I could just see him once more. If only I could tell him once again that I love him. If only I could give him one last hug. If only . . . If only . . .

"Mary, dear, My plan is perfect for you, and for Steve. His life is complete. All the days ordained for him have been completed. Steve is far happier now than he would be hiking the beautiful hills."

We completed the arrangements for Steve's burial plot and drove home in the gathering dusk, dazed, disbelieving, heartsore.

More friends and family gathered for dinner, and the evening passed making plans for the memorial service, talking about the murder, and trying to comfort one another. Most of the conversations were conducted in a murmur, as though by speaking very quietly the subject might somehow disappear. But in spite of the muted voices, the harsh reality screamed its presence.

We gathered with our daughters and their husbands many times that day to pray together, to cry together, to talk. As Kathy and Dave were leaving that evening to return to their own home, Jerry and I and our daughters stood in a circle with our arms around one another, our heads bowed and touching. As we prayed I watched our mingled tears dripping on our shoes.

Lord, why do my girls have to suffer like this? It's enough that Jerry and I are torn, but I feel so badly for my girls. They have to go through the rest of their lives without a brother. Help them, please. Comfort them. Ease their hurt.

Oh, Lord, we miss Steve so much. How can we live a lifetime without him? Please, couldn't we go to Heaven now, too? No, I know we can't do that, but this hurts so much. Please give Steve a hug today. Tell him we're so sorry he was murdered. Tell him we're sorry we didn't get to say goodbye. Tell him we love him. We'll see him again soon. Help us here. This pain is so terrible.

Late that evening Ruth arrived after a long flight from Kenya. In those prolonged night hours of flying, she prayed and reflected on Steve's life and what his sudden, violent death would mean to our total family. Fatigued, mourning, and jet-lagged, she arrived, and oh, how good it was to see her, to embrace, to weep together, to share the burden of our terrible grief.

As the household quieted, Jerry and I closed our bedroom door. Numb with grief and shock, we lay down to weep and pray and doze, and awaken to weep again.

Chapter 4

VIEWING THE BODY

The days between Steve's murder and funeral blended into a collage of sorrow, pain, sleepless nights, and frantic activity.

The constant presence of family and friends helped a great deal to alleviate thoughts that were too terrible to bear. Throughout Sunday and Monday other friends and family continued to arrive by car and plane. We were touched by the effort people made from all over the country to come and be with us, to tell us of their care and concern and sorrow.

My brothers and their families came. Lyla, my brother's wife and my close friend since early childhood, said, "Oh, Mary," as she entered the house and enfolded me in a weeping embrace. All of the sorrow she felt for me was embodied in those two words. Surrounded by her own three strong sons, she expressed the suffering and anguish of one mother's heart to another.

I found such a help in being enveloped by my extended family—my brothers, my sisters, their families, Jerry's brothers and cousins who had traveled long distances to be with us. One of Jerry's brothers, Richard, came from Europe where he makes his home. Their very presence spoke of their sorrow and their sympathy, and reassured us of their care and support during those days. It is not easy to be in the presence of excruciating pain in another person, and they joined in our tears, the repetitions of the murder story, and our palpable sadness.

WHERE WERE YOU WHEN THE NEWS CAME?

Family and friends wanted to share how they had heard of Steve's murder, how they responded, the grief and outrage they felt when they first heard the news.

My older brother, Sam, was teaching in his fifth-grade classroom when he was summoned to the phone. After hearing the terrible account of Steve's death, the school secretary suggested he return home for the rest of the day. He assured her he would be fine and returned to his class. As he started to speak to his students, he broke down and had to leave the room. His team teachers insisted he leave for the day.

My friend Jean went to pick up her children at school. When they didn't come out right away, she went to the office.

The secretary said, "Isn't it terrible about the Whites' son?"

"What happened? I haven't heard anything."

"He was murdered."

Jean returned to her car, weeping and dazed. Other family members and friends told us of their deep shock and disbelief when first confronted with the news. As they arrived, all remained incredulous at the news of Steve's shocking murder. Most of us had never known a murder victim and had no contact with murder other than impersonal news reports.

After the trip to the mortuary, we began to talk about the funeral. Julie graciously gave us great freedom to help plan the service. She asked for our advice and suggestions. Who should sing? What Scripture readings? Should *we* say anything? Jerry and I knew that we would like Lorne Sanny, longtime president of The Navigators and close personal friend, to speak. But what a difficult thing to ask a dear friend to do.

My emotional response was to hold the memorial service as soon as possible, to get it over with. I longed to pull a Rip Van Winkle act, to fall asleep and wake up in five years with the pain gone. How could I plan a funeral for my son? What an appalling and impossible assignment.

As we forced ourselves to discuss details, I gradually responded to the opportunity to make the event a memorable time of appreciation for Steve's life and gratitude to God for His promise of *eternal* life.

Slowly the plans came together. All of the friends we asked to participate through music or speaking readily agreed, a kindness that helped make the thought of the funeral more bearable.

A PRIVATE VIEWING

The day before Steve's burial, we finally made a decision about viewing his body. The detectives urged us not to go, saying that in their experience families who viewed a body following a homicide generally regretted it. However, the funeral director insisted that Steve's appearance was fine and that his mortal wounds did not impair his face in any way.

The sheriff's department released Steve's body following the autopsy. The only details we knew at that time were that three shots had been fired at point-blank range into the back of Steve's head, severing his spinal cord.

Marty, a nurse, and her husband, Jay, offered to view Steve's body first to let us know if they felt it would be good for us to go. They returned from the mortuary saying they had found no discernible injury. They felt if we could handle the emotional impact, they would encourage us to go.

As much as I dreaded seeing my beloved son in a

casket, I felt compelled to go. I had to *know* that Steve had died. I felt in some dim way that seeing Steve's body would bring reality to the shocking news of his death. Not every family member felt as I did, and some chose not to attend the viewing, preferring to remember Steve when he was alive.

Only family members and a few close friends went to the mortuary for the viewing. As much as possible we wanted to preserve a measure of dignity and decorum in spite of the gruesome details of the murder. We felt if we announced public calling hours, curious people would come and possibly reduce the sense of respect we wanted to maintain.

As I entered that small viewing room with Jerry's supporting arm around me and Kristie holding my hand, feelings of great dread swept over me. I had seen dead bodies before. We had buried all of our parents and had attended many funeral services, but nothing prepares a parent to see the lifeless body of a beloved child in a casket.

Julie had chosen casual clothes for Steve—a favorite sweater and a pair of casual slacks, very much in keeping with his approach to life. He looked so peaceful, rather like he was lying on a couch enjoying a midday nap. As promised, I saw no signs of injury, but I knew that behind his familiar, serene face was a ruined skull wantonly destroyed by a murderer's bullets. Tears streaming, I moved closer.

"Steve. My dear Steve," I murmured, wanting to reach out and gather him close.

God, give me strength. My precious son, in a casket. This is so excruciatingly painful. I don't know if I can stand it. Is there no way we can have Steve back? Do we have to go on without him? Couldn't I have him

41

back for just five minutes? I didn't get to say goodbye. I want so much to give him just one more hug. I need to look into his eyes once again. My only son is lying here dead, cut down and destroyed for no reason or purpose.

"Remember, Mary, he is with Me. He is at peace. He is joyful. He will never know pain again."

But there's so much I don't know, God. Did he suffer? I can't bear the thought that he suffered, that he was frightened, that he was alone when he died.

"My dear, he wasn't alone. I was with him. I am with you right now. I will never leave you nor forsake you."

But, murder, Lord? No one can know what it feels like to know Steve was murdered.

"My dear Mary. I know what you feel. I know how hard it is. Remember, My Son, too, was murdered."

Oh, yes, God, that's right. Jesus was murdered. He, too, was innocent. Another Mary felt as I do now. Another mother wept for her precious Son, but she watched His death. At least I am seeing Steve now with his dear face intact and peaceful, not suffering.

And with that assurance came a tiny release from the consuming ache of loss. I felt a vast weakness flood over me and leaned gratefully into Jerry.

Six months after Steve's death, dear friends of ours lost their youngest son in an early morning motorcycle accident. He was riding to work when, blinded by the rising sun, he crashed headlong into a moving pickup truck. That mother told me that when she entered the viewing room to see his body, she sank to the floor. She had no sensation of strength leaving her limbs, but suddenly found herself on the floor. Her family helped her to a chair, and after a brief rest she rose again, only to have the same response as she fell to the floor a second time.

Although I didn't fall when I saw Steve's body, I did sense a consuming weakness as I was faced with the crushing reality of his death. Thoughts about the autopsy entered my mind, but I shoved them aside. As a family we drew together and held one another. We prayed. I couldn't remember the words five minutes later, but I did feel a measure of peace and acceptance.

In twos, threes, and small groups, family and friends went into the viewing room after us. Kristie went in again, alone, to say a final, private goodbye to her big brother. As we left the funeral home, I took a last lingering look at Steve's body through the open door to the viewing room. I was crushed with the feeling that I was deserting him, leaving him alone, abandoned.

I remember nothing about the rest of that day, and my journal for that time records nothing. The shock of seeing Steve's body drove rational thought from my mind. I moved through the rest of the day automatically, not seeing, not thinking, reacting only by habit and instinct, helped along by my patient family and friends.

Chapter 5

STRETCHER BEARERS FOR THE FIRST DAYS OF GRIEF

An avalanche of kindness flowed toward us from the moment friends, neighbors, and colleagues, and even strangers, heard of Steve's murder.

Jerry was my strength during those terrible days. He is, by nature, kind and patient and supportive, but the unflagging compassion he showed to me during that time could only have come from his deep relationship with God. I will always be grateful for the way he so generously shared his strength with me.

From the moment he enfolded me in his arms in the motel and told me the terrible news, he was a fortress of comfort, caring, and common sense.

He, too, had lost his firstborn, his only son, his future hopes. Yet in his own agonizing pain, he offered me his strength and comfort. He gently directed my thoughts toward God. He showed his vulnerability as he cried with me. He prayed for me; he prayed with me.

He patiently listened to my endless recital of futile questions as I painfully speculated on the details of Steve's murder. He continually reassured me that our daughters and Julie would be safe. He answered phone call after phone call when I could not summon the energy to talk with relatives and friends. And all the while he confirmed his love for me in many ways, he functioned capably in the many decisions that had to be made, and made quickly.

As I watched Jerry move through those days, my heart broke for him. I knew the profound mourning that gripped him even as he made decisions, talked endlessly on the phone, consulted with the funeral director, spoke with the media, and comforted his daughters and Julie and me.

I, alone, in the privacy of our bedroom, heard him

sob brokenly as he cried, "I'll never see him again. I'll never see him again." I, alone, knew of his sleepless nights, his sadness, his longings for his son.

Jerry drew strength from his deep trust in God and our love for each other. Both of us found help and strength from friendships of many years' standing. Close friends rushed to be with us when they heard of Steve's murder.

FRIENDS WHO STOOD BY US

For several years we had counted three couples among our dearest friends. Two couples lived in Seattle, and the third in Chico, California. In spite of the geographical distances that separated us, we met several times a year for friendship, spiritual stimulation, and personal accountability. We kept in close touch the rest of the time.

A few years before Steve's death we agreed together to *be there* for one another in any serious need. We all harbored the idea that the need would be the death of one of us, or a serious financial setback, or a problem that would need the counsel and rebuke of close and trusted friends. Never did we imagine the murder of one of our children.

Fred Hignell, in Chico, was attending a business meeting when he received the news. He immediately left the meeting, drove directly to the small Chico airport, and was allowed to board a flight without a ticket. The aircraft was ready to leave, but after hearing Fred's hurried explanation, airline personnel said, "Get on, get on; we'll issue a ticket in Salt Lake."

Kaylinn, at home with their two small sons, made plans to arrive later.

Chris and Alice Canlis, owners of a premier restaurant in Seattle, also heard the news of Steve's murder during a business meeting. Chris left immediately for the airport. Alice made flight reservations, packed, and drove to Karen and Tim's apartment, airline tickets in hand, and traveled with them to Colorado Springs.

Stan and Lois Newell heard the news at their Seattle office where Stan conducts a busy podiatry practice. He completed his appointments for the day, then he and Lois boarded an airplane to come as quickly as they could, arriving late in the evening.

How good it was to feel their arms around us, to hear their assurances of love. With an unspoken awareness, they began to support and organize and help us plan for the days ahead. They, together with dear local friends, devoted eighteen-hour days to helping with the endless details we had to face.

Fred became our right hand as he listed all ideas, suggestions, and plans in the notebook that never seemed to leave his hand. Occasionally he interjected an idea or question, gently directing our thoughts to possibilities. He stayed with us during interviews with the police and the media. He entered the mortuary viewing room with us. His help never seemed like interference, only a strong rock for us to lean on when our distraught minds refused to function.

Chris and Alice and Lois worked tirelessly in the kitchen preparing and serving an endless supply of food. Much of the food came from friends, neighbors, and church members. Individuals and groups ebbed and flowed through the house, and most of them stopped awhile to eat or at least to drink coffee.

Stan answered the doorbell as it rang again and

again for flower deliveries, visits from supportive friends, and the arrival of telegrams. He mowed the lawn and played with the grandchildren. He ran errands and answered the phone. After the heavy snowfall, he wryly remarked, "If I had known it was going to snow, I wouldn't have bothered to mow the lawn!"

These unselfish efforts on our behalf freed us to grieve, to talk with those who came to offer sympathy, to rest and to plan. Perhaps their greatest gift to us was their presence. They were willing to stand with us in our anguish, to remove whatever pressures they could, to help, listen, love, and cry.

We received this same love and sympathy from our local friends. They worked tirelessly to help in those frantic days following Steve's murder.

A good friend and Navigator colleague, Doug Sparks, arrived to offer his sympathy and help. Only a year before, Doug's daughter and her husband had been killed in a horrific head-on car collision with a drunken driver. Doug's little grandson was grievously injured in the accident and the prognosis for his recovery remained doubtful. We had watched Doug and his family go through that terrible time, unable to fully comprehend the sorrow in his family. And now he came to offer his comfort and empathy to us.

"Doug, you know just how we feel," Jerry said to him as he arrived.

"No, Jerry, I don't really. Only God knows how you truly feel."

That wise observation provided us with a mindset that strengthened us in the days and weeks ahead. Even with all of the love and compassion and caring that enveloped us, only God fully knew the depth of our grief and emptiness.

Many colleagues and friends arrived every day to help. In my dazed grief, I missed much of what they did, but the household would not have run without their help. They cleaned and cooked and washed clothes. Many people were eating in our home during those days. Paper plates and cups were used to facilitate cleanup. My friend, Carol, carried away huge trash bags filled with the remains. Another night she left chocolate bars on everyone's pillow as a loving reminder of her concern. Ignoring personal fatigue and inconvenience, these friends gave generously of their time and energy.

Refrigerator space remained at a premium. In desperation, Alice and Lois stored juice and soft drinks in the snow that had formed into drifts on the back patio. Many such creative innovations took place in the kitchen during those days of heavy guest traffic and extra family members in the house.

Although Stan had shoveled the walk and the drive after the snow began, it continued to fall. Early the next morning, a friend from church arrived in his truck, shoveled the walk, and drove away without our knowledge. Only later did someone tell us of his unselfish act of kindness. Many such anonymous actions took place during those hectic, grieving days as loving friends reached out to lift our burden in practical, caring ways.

THE COMFORT OF INNOCENTS

During those achingly sad days I was immeasurably helped by seeing and holding my little grandsons. Michael was only two, his brother Daniel just a little tad of eight months, and Jerad ten months. They provided an aura of vitality and energy that gave a lovely, hopeful contrast to the atmosphere of death and grief permeating our lives.

Receiving their spontaneous affection calmed my spirit and brought a sense of hope to me. Holding their little bodies brought back memories of Steve at that age. God had given Steve thirty years of life on earth. As I embraced the little boys I thought often of the prospect of a full and happy lifetime ahead of them.

Oh God, please protect these precious, innocent babies. Shield them with Your love. Send Your angels to watch over them. Spare my dear daughters from ever knowing the dreadful sorrow of losing a beloved child.

Those precious children brought smiles and even laughter to the grieving people around them. Jerad was a husky, chubby baby, always ready to eat whatever was offered to him. Daniel, on the other hand, was far more selective in his eating choices and needed coaxing to accept food his mother chose for him.

Seated in separate highchairs in the kitchen, Jerad would finish eating long before Daniel. He watched with great interest as the food-laden spoon continued to hover around Daniel's face, waiting for his mouth to open. In sympathetic reaction and anticipation, Jerad's mouth would open wide, hoping perhaps that Daniel's spoon would take a detour across the kitchen to his own mouth. Jerad's intent focus on that spoon brought much laughter to the watching adults.

OUR STRETCHER BEARERS

Flowers flooded the house, beautiful bouquets and plants covering tables, dresser tops, and even the floor. People arrived with casseroles and fresh bread and cakes. Baskets containing fruit and specialty coffees appeared on the front step. Dozens of phone calls offered help of every kind.

Sympathetic faxes flowed in from around the world. The phone rang endlessly with callers expressing their shock and grief in broken tones. Friends arrived to embrace us and leave quickly or sometimes sit silently with us, sharing our suffering.

We will never know all of the effort, love, concern, and help that flowed our way through those days. Many people brought food and slipped away without leaving their names. Others worked behind the scenes making calls, setting up the church for the memorial service, arranging housing and transportation for the many family members and friends who arrived from a distance. All prayed for us. We felt carried along on the love and prayers of friends as we functioned beyond our capacity during those terrible days.

Local friends, beloved friends of many years' standing, spent hours helping and sympathizing, grieving with us. The number of friends who expressed deep anger over the senselessness of the murder amazed me. My shock and grief remained so overwhelming that I had no capacity for anger.

On a dim level, I knew I did not have the emotional energy to be angry and to grieve at the same time. But there was a sense of comfort that friends recognized the great injustice of Steve's death and were willing to state their rage.

Their anger struck me as *righteous indignation*, a solid abhorrence for the act that deliberately destroyed an innocent human life. The murder was incomprehensible to me. Often as I was talking with a friend or family member during those early days, a great wave of bewilderment flooded through me. My mind closed down as I tried to comprehend Steve's senseless murder. Grief, painful and overpowering, blocked logical thought. I could find no rationale to explain such a reprehensible, cruel act.

Chapter 6

THE COMMITTAL SERVICE

The day of Steve's funeral dawned bleak — overcast and cold. May 1. Ruth's birthday. May Day. Spring should be in full bloom, warm and fragrant. Instead, the dismal weather mirrored my dread of the day before me. As I arose, I could sense the toll relentless grief had taken on my body. I felt battered and weak. Days of little food, even less sleep, and pounding, pitiless mourning had drained my energy, leaving me spent and shaky.

Dear God, do we have to bury Steve today? Can't we wait? I don't know if I can bear it if we put his body in the ground. It's too cold. Too cold. It will really be over. How can I say goodbye on a day like this? I can't. I can't. Please, somebody. Please, wait. Maybe tomorrow I can bear it. Maybe tomorrow I'll be strong enough. Lord, help me.

And then the sweet reassurance from God.

"Yes, My dear, you can bear it. I will be with you. I will send My angels to be in charge of you today. They will bear you up. My strength is made perfect in your weakness. Don't let your heart be troubled. Don't let it be afraid. I am with you always."

Kaylinn urged me to eat, and I did try, but it was impossible to force food past the lump in my throat. I drank the orange juice she gave me. Alice helped me choose something to wear.

The morning hours blurred, punctuated with moments of pain and joy. Jerry holding me in a strengthening embrace . . . Ruth practicing a few songs for a piano postlude for the memorial service . . . laughter over little Jerad's baby antics . . . prayer with the family . . . loving embraces . . . friends arriving . . . and always, the sharp, agonizing images of Steve's body in the casket.

56

Jerry and I continued to work on a letter from the family that Tim would read at the memorial service. We wanted it to be warm without being maudlin, and to give a sense of Steve's life and our deep loss while expressing our faith in God's comfort and good plan.

Michael climbed into my arms, asking, "Are you sad, Nana?" as he saw my tears streaming.

"Yes, I am, my darling," I answered him. "Because I miss Uncle Steve so much. But Jesus will help us."

He wound his little arms around my neck, hugging me, offering comfort in the only way he knew how in the confusing maelstrom of adult grief swirling around him. How precious those little arms felt, living bands of innocent comfort strengthening me for the day ahead.

Friends and family arrived to lunch together and organize transportation to the cemetery. Candid photos taken during that meal show somber, stressed faces. We planned a committal service first, then a memorial service later in the day when more people would be off work.

We ate, then circled together to pray for strength and comfort. I leaned heavily into Jerry, slumping into his supporting arms. Marty, seeing my weakness, grabbed some crackers and fruit, stuffing them into her purse in case I fainted.

Bundled in winter coats and warm gloves, we left at last for the cemetery. We made no public announcement regarding this graveside service. We felt the presence of reporters or television cameras might weaken our opportunity to say goodbye to Steve in privacy and quiet reverence.

I sat in the back of the van with Ruth on one side and Kristie on the other. Both held my hands for strength and comfort as we drove to the cemetery. I felt drained, empty, unaware.

Halfway there we passed a filling station where a taxi was parked at the gas pumps. The sight of that yellow car jerked me from my lethargy and lacerated my heart.

"Oh, God," I cried out.

"What is it, Mom? What's wrong?" Kristie asked me.

"It's a yellow cab." I pointed. "God, please protect that cab driver." My tears began to flow.

I felt Ruth's and Kristie's hands tighten on mine. In silence we drove the rest of the way.

The funeral director led us to a few chairs placed in the snow near the gravesite. Julie sat between Jerry and me as our daughters and other family members and friends circled the grave. I was filled with a sense of unreality, a disbelief that I was attending my only son's funeral.

My head down, I was suddenly aware of a slight commotion in front of me. Looking up through my tears I saw six young men bearing his casket toward the portable bier in front of me. Involuntarily I moaned aloud.

Oh, God. I forgot there would be a casket. How could I forget? My dear Steve. You are in there. No. God, no. This can't be true. My precious son. I can't bear this.

I moaned again. Swiftly Fred knelt in the snow beside my chair. He began to whisper to me.

"The Lord is my shepherd. I shall not want. He maketh me to lie down in green pastures, He leadeth me beside the still waters, He restoreth my soul."

As he spoke the timeless words of Psalm 23, I felt

calmness and strength flood through me. My tears still flowed and the agony of losing Steve remained strong, but my panic and desperation receded.

A RESURRECTION REMINDER

Jay, a pastor and army chaplain, conducted the brief service. As he read Scripture, reviewed Steve's obituary, and prayed, I clung to the fragment of Scripture Fred had offered. Surrounded by family and friends, I was only dimly aware of the words Jay spoke.

Midway through the brief service we heard the singing of a bird. High overhead, in the still bare branches of an elm tree, a lone bird sang a beautiful buoyant melody in sharp contrast to the stark melancholy below. Later I learned that such an incident is not uncommon. Grieving families often report unusual appearances of birds, butterflies, small animals. Are such happenings a message from God? They do serve to bring a measure of comfort and hope to those who mourn.

I found a special consolation in offering Julie a bit of comfort, putting my arm around her and feeling Jerry's arm encircling her sobbing body from the other side. I felt a fresh wave of grief for her as I thought of her lonely, uncertain days ahead.

At the end of the service Jay read a special statement we had prepared.

"At Eastertime, Steve gave bouquets of tulips to Julie and Mary. Tulips remind us of new life and renewal in springtime. In the confident hope of eternal life and seeing Steve again, the family would like to return the loving gesture Steve made to us."

Julie and I stepped forward and placed bouquets

of tulips on the casket. Then Kathy, Karen, and Kristie, too, came forward with tulips. A final poignant tribute to Steve in memory of his last gifts to us.

As the service ended, our friends drifted toward the waiting cars. Reluctantly, slowly, I approached the casket for the last time. I felt totally drained, terribly tired, filled with an overwhelming sadness. I let my gloved hand rest on the casket for a long moment. But as Jerry put his arm around me and led me away, my hand slipped from the smooth walnut wood and I felt a fresh surge of loss.

Dear God, I can't leave him here. I can't abandon him like this. He shouldn't have to stay here alone. It's so cold and lonely here. He's all by himself. Everyone is leaving. I can't leave him alone.

"My dear, he isn't alone, he's with Me. He's not there. He's happier than you could ever imagine. He is not lonely. He is not alone. He's warm, he's happy, he's alive, and he's content. He's with Me."

Chapter 7

THE MEMORIAL SERVICE

After a silent drive, we arrived at the church for the 4:00 p.m. service. Although the church normally housed a school during the weekdays, the administration dismissed the students early so the building would be quiet for the memorial service.

Someone had thoughtfully prepared a room for our family to use as we waited for the service to begin. Comfortable couches, refreshments, and warm drinks awaited us for the short interlude before the service began. We brushed our windblown hair, nibbled a few cookies, and tried to relax for a few moments.

We had asked Kristie's violin teacher, concertmaster of the local symphony, to play some of our favorite hymns and Steve's favorite songs before the service began. As friends and family slipped in and out of the room, I could hear those beautiful strains floating from the auditorium.

At last our family was led to the front row of the sanctuary. I was only dimly aware of the hundreds of people who had come to mourn with us. Flowers lined the platform, vivid reminders of people's love for us and their remembrance of Steve. Julie, her parents, Jerry, and I sat on the front row. Our family filled the next several rows.

I wanted to reach out to my daughters and fold them to me, but they were seated behind me. I strongly sensed the love and support and prayers from those who had come to the church and from people around the world, whose prayers poured toward us at that moment.

Jay opened the service, thanking all who had come to share in our sorrow and to remember Steve. We rose to sing the powerful words of the ancient hymn "Immortal, Invisible, God Only Wise." I tried to

62

join in but found my voice breaking and could only listen to the hundreds of voices around me rising in the beautiful words of the song.

Julie's father presented some remarks about Steve's life. He referred to Steve's peaceloving and simple lifestyle, his search for truth and meaning, his love of people, and his joy of the outdoors. In a final statement that deeply touched me, he said that Steve would never leave our hearts.

A good friend read a letter Julie had written expressing her deep sorrow.

My dearest Stephen,

I did so love you. Our years together were both tumultuous and beautiful. Since learning about your senseless passing, a steady stream of memories and emotions roll through my mind, sometimes all jumbled up, other times crystal clear.

I remember when I first met you in Spanish class. You were so shy and I was unapproachable. Slowly, while conjugating verbs and struggling with pronunciations, you won my heart with your sweet smiles and gentle manner. I remember the fun times we had cross-country skiing. With our dogs close at our heels we laughed and enjoyed our time together. I remember our picture-perfect wedding that glorious day in September, buying our house and working to fix it up. I also remember lying awake at nights, alone, while you drove your cab. I wondered where you were, if you were safe, and when you were coming home.

My emotions are much harder to handle. I feel so incredibly sorry for you. There is no rationale behind what happened to you. Did you know what was going on in those last few minutes? I feel anger. Why did you choose to live on the edge of danger? Did you ever consider the possibilities? And how your death would affect the people who loved you? Every day you took a needless risk. You never should have been there. I feel guilt—a lot of guilt—the times I pressured you and withheld the support you so desperately needed. The unkind things I said to you. If only there were a way to take them back. I miss you and love you. I wanted so much for us to be happy and content and grow old together.

It is only after your passing that I realize all I learned from you. I wonder what lasting things from you I can keep dear to me for the rest of my life. Your caring warmth for all people—no matter what. Your gracious giving nature—those kind gestures you went out of your way to do. Your faith in humankind that people will treat you fairly if that's how you treat them. These are the qualities I want to remember and embody in myself. I only wish I had fully utilized them while you were here. Oh, how we take the ones we are closest to for granted.

You are gone now. I must pick up all these fragments, pull them together, and live by what I have learned from you. You can be sure, Stephen, that no matter what my future holds, I will always love and remember you. There is a part of my heart and soul that belongs to only you.

In the few days preceding Steve's funeral, Jerry and I had talked often of what we wanted to convey to others regarding Steve—our feelings, family memories, and the comfort and grace of God. After many revisions (unlike Julie, who wrote her beautiful tribute in one sitting), we asked Tim to read the following reflections from us.

On behalf of Julie, the Cass family, and all of us in the White family, thank you for coming to share our pain and grief, and especially to remember and honor Steve.

We want to share a few family remembrances of Steve and also to share how we view the future.

We were blessed with thirty wonderful years with Steve. We remember his learning to read at age two and a half. His first reader was "I Learn How to Read about Jesus." At three and a half he did simple math, so when he began kindergarten, he found it a bit redundant.

He brought us much joy and laughter with his wry sense of humor, his love for the outdoors from his youth on up. Growing up at the Air Force Academy was like having his own private park. We hiked in the mountains, once to Blodgett Peak, discovering an old World War II plane wreck. He and Julie loved the mountains— hiking, camping, skiing.

Early in his life at the Academy, he made a personal commitment to receive Jesus Christ as his Savior. With his good mind and intellect, it was not just a childhood act. And he affirmed it many times again. In his late teens and twenties, he wrestled with many questions—the poor and justice, the hypocrisy that he saw. But just last

June, on Jerry's birthday, in a long drive in the mountains with us, he said, "I'm taking a leap of faith to seek God."

In 1983 Steve brought Julie to meet us in Seattle. In 1984 we welcomed this beautiful, creative woman into our family as our daughter-in-law. We love her very deeply.

Steve deeply loved his sisters and was very protective of them. They share many fond memories. We remember that wry sense of humor even in those childhood days. At our home, when conflict came, the children were asked to say something nice about each other. On one occasion, after a long pause, Steve said, "She has a wonderful brother."

Kathy remembers, while she was growing up, that Steve understood her fears and was careful never to criticize or ridicule her. Instead, he was gentle and reassuring. One week before Steve's death, Kathy left a message with the cab company for Steve to call her. Instead of calling, he came over to her house. They sat in the kitchen for an hour or so and had a deep heart to heart conversation. Kathy told him that she loved him and supported him in his decisions. She knew that he loved her.

When they were young, Karen always felt secure when Steve was there. She would often awaken at midnight, smell tater tots and pizza, knowing Steve was there having his midnight snack. She could roll over secure and go to sleep. Coming home from college a few years ago, Steve took her to a picnic at Bear Creek Park, overlooking the city. They sat and talked as friends.

Just a month ago, Karen called him and left a message to call back. He walked out of a concert he was covering for KRCC and immediately called. Instant response to his sister.

Kris recalls when she was five and Steve fifteen, he would take her to the park while he played basketball with his friends and she would play at the kiddy playground. When he was ready to go home, he would whistle, she would come, and he would walk her home, holding her hand, paying no attention to the kidding of his friends about his little sister.

Kristie went to Steve and Julie's house last summer to house-sit. She and Steve started talking. Steve began to help her put things in her life into perspective as to why she was like she was, in her personality and in the family. He said he understood her. Kris felt that he really did. He was hard on her, giving her a "big brother" talk. He said he had planned to say these things in a few years but decided to do it now.

He dearly loved Kathy, Karen, and Kristie and would give his life for them. In some ways, perhaps he did.

But now, what of the future? What about the "whys" of this sad time?

We do not have all the answers. We feel such deep pain and grief as parents and sisters. We cry till there are no more tears, and then we cry some more.

But in this overwhelming grief, we have a tremendous hope. This hope is that real life does not end with physical death. Jesus said, "I am the resurrection and the life. He who believes in me will live, even though he dies; and whoever lives and believes in me will never die." There is more to life than just being alive.

Steve had little interest in materialism, money, and things. Our hope is in a real Christ, who lived in real history and died a far worse death. And He rose from the dead. This is the hope that gives us peace in all this pain.

It is not a pie-in-the-sky hope. Or an emotional crutch. It is as real as the body we live in every day. But without Christ, the future would be hopeless.

This morning we read the Bible together and read a passage that God used to communicate to us about all our family. "The children of your servants will live in your presence; their descendants will be established before you. Praise the Lord, O my soul. All my inmost being, praise his holy name. Praise the Lord, O my soul, and forget not all his benefits . . . who redeems your life from the pit and crowns you with love and compassion."

Today Steve is in the presence of Jesus Christ with all his questions answered. And we have that as our certain assurance to go on in the future.

Music has always been an important part of our family life. The day before the memorial service, our three daughters, who all have lovely singing voices, recorded a song written by Kathy's former music director. The words spoke exactly what we felt. And the message of the song reflected, I felt, the thoughts Steve would have as well. As our daughters' clear, beautiful voices floated across the auditorium from the public address system, I felt a measure of consolation in the message of the song.

I don't understand why some people must suffer
or why children and young people die.
I don't understand why some people have plenty
while others just barely get by.
Why do new waves of trouble keep pounding around me
before yesterday's waves ebb away?
But in moments like these when my faith starts to falter
God's Spirit just tenderly whispers to say:
There's a reason; There's a plan
There's a purpose and there's a goal
But Jesus who loves us more than anyone can
Is still very much in control.
When the tracks that I'm leaving don't follow the path
that I thought that they would take
When the things that I'm achieving don't make quite
the impact
that I thought that they would make,
When I daily encounter disruption and strife
to achieve what's expected of me
I recall that God is at work in my life
using trials to polish His image in me.
There's a reason; There's a plan
There's a purpose and there's a goal
But Jesus who loves us more than anyone can
Is still very much in control.[1]

Laura Davis, a fellow church member with a beautiful voice, sang of hope for the future and trust in God when she sang, "Because He Lives, I Can Face Tomorrow."[2]

God, somehow we will all face tomorrow with Your

help. I know You will be there for us. Give us strength right now, please, as we say goodbye to our Steve. Help us to honor You in what is said and done here today.

Lorne Sanny, longtime president of The Navigators and a dear personal friend, presented a powerful and thought-provoking message. He used the Old Testament passage of Ecclesiastes 7:2-4 as a text.

It is better to go to a house of mourning than to go to a house of feasting, for death is the destiny of every man; the living should take this to heart. Sorrow is better than laughter, because a sad face is good for the heart. The heart of the wise is in the house of mourning, but the heart of fools is in the house of pleasure.

Lorne began his remarks with an illustration: "Deep grief is like a lump of lead down inside that feels like it will never leave. But in time it will dissolve. The place where it was will heal. But that place will never be filled. It will always be empty. And in this case, that's Steve's place. It will always be there. And we wouldn't have it any other way. Others may come into our lives, but not into that place."

He went on, "A cloud hangs over Steve's funeral like no other I have ever attended. We feel the shock and horror of the crime. We are angry at the hideous evil that commits murder. It brings home to us that the Bible is right. 'The heart of man is deceitful above all things and desperately wicked.' There must be a judgment. There will be a judgment. But that doesn't comfort us much, as true as it is."

Lorne emphasized the injustice of Steve's death,

the uncertainty of life, and the need to review the serious nature of eternity. He spoke clearly of the confidence we can have in a relationship with God through His Son, Jesus. My tears dried and my mind cleared as I listened to his wise words.

As Jay closed the service with prayer, I felt as though a chapter in my life was ending, as indeed it was. Although I didn't fully understand it, another door was opening that would lead to endless days of painful sorrow and slow, slow recovery to hope and healing.

Jerry and I remained at the front of the auditorium following the service to greet people who came to offer us their sympathy and support. The line went on and on, and I sensed a swelling gratitude to all the people who wanted to share our pain—Steve's friends, our friends, Navigator staff, Steve's coworkers from the taxi company and the radio station, church members, relatives.

Many had come from distant places for the memorial service. Some waited in line nearly an hour to embrace us, weep with us, and whisper a few words of comfort. At one point I looked up and saw the long line of people patiently standing in the aisle waiting to talk with us. Many were crying. They will never know how much their supportive presence meant to us that day.

A GOD-SENT MESSENGER

A few days before the funeral I had asked Ruth, a gifted pianist, if she would play a piano postlude. At first she said no. Although stalwart in spirit, she felt too fragile emotionally to do it. But after some consideration, she said she would like to honor Steve's memory in that way. As long as she didn't look at me and see my tears, she felt she could play.

As she played, she noticed a very large man standing near the piano, arms folded across his chest, carefully watching the audience. Jerry, too, noticed him, as did our son-in-law Dave. His demeanor and expression were so solemn and unusual that finally Jerry went to speak to him.

"Hello. I'm Jerry White, Steve's dad. Are you a friend of Steve's?"

"No."

"Are you with the police?" We had been told that plainclothes detectives would be in the audience.

"No."

"What brings you here today?"

"I am here to see that no harm will come to this family."

This peculiar response puzzled Jerry, but more people came to speak with him and he was quickly enveloped again in conversations with others.

Dave, too, spoke with the man and received the same answers. Dave did ask for his name, and later, in checking for someone of that name and description, we found no one.

Was the man a God-sent angel? Or was he a local community member so incensed by Steve's brutal murder that he came to be a part of the final remembrance of Steve? Was he a self-appointed guardian of the remaining family members?

I prefer to think that he was God-sent, a symbol of God's love and care for us as a family, a sign of comfort and safety and encouragement. He drifted away as obscurely as he had come. No one saw him arrive and no one saw him leave. Although our family has mixed ideas about his presence and purpose that day, I choose to believe he was a messenger from God, if for no other reason than to give us a sense of security and protection.

At last we left the church in the growing cold of early evening. We arrived home to find nearly one hundred friends and family gathered for a meal together, a meal provided by the generosity of church and Navigator friends. We received, again, the support and caring that had come to mean so much.

Gradually the house cleared, we talked at length with the family members who had come from a distance, and finally, overwhelmed with exhaustion, Jerry and I dropped into bed. Weeping, clinging together, we prayed as we waited for the sleeping pills to take effect.

God, thank You for the strength to get through this day. Please comfort our girls and dear Julie tonight. How can they bear this? How can any of us bear it? Give us strength for the road ahead. We miss Steve so much. Only You can help us.

NOTES
1. "There's a Reason," words and music by Dan Foster. Copyright by Ron Harris Music, all rights reserved, used by permission.
2. "Because He Lives," Gloria and William J. Gaither, *The Hymnal for Worship and Celebration*, Word Music, Waco, Texas,© 1986.

Chapter 8

THE HEALING PROCESS BEGINS

Now began the long, painful process of healing. Not forgetting. Never forgetting. Could a mother ever forget her child? Can the pain of living without a loved one be forgotten? Should good memories be put aside? Never. But healing, yes. That terrible, painful process must begin.

The days settled into an endless routine of pressing inner pain, a struggle to return to some form of normalcy in daily life. The excruciating process of adjusting to Steve's death led to neverending, crushing, heartbreaking anguish. At times it seemed unbearable, and death would have been a welcome release from the ceaseless sorrow. But in spite of the grief, we tried to assume a normal facade and fit into that unlikely mode.

No one can predict or prescribe healing for another. Each healing is as unique as the person going through it. Each day is unpredictable. Each night brings the oblivion of troubled sleep, and each awakening brings renewed pain and sorrow.

Body, mind, and spirit—all are severely wounded through grief. All need healing. Each part of the human body and soul needs restoration and renewal. It takes time, a very long, painful time.

The days following the funeral were heavy with unending mourning punctuated with flurries of necessary activity. The fallout from Steve's murder and funeral included continued visits with the police, streams of visitors wanting to share our grief, stacks of mail, and the ever-present struggle to return to normal life, although we knew that normal would never be the same again. A long arduous road to wholeness lay ahead of us.

Jerry and I felt ill-equipped to face the heavy

demands of that time. We were tired, so tired. In a matter of days energy, motivation, and vitality had drained away, leaving us reeling with fatigue and sorrow.

Demands flooded in and we didn't know where to begin. Two of Jerry's colleagues came every morning to listen and talk. They assessed his personal frame of mind, reported on the happenings in the office, and offered insightful counsel on Jerry's return to his responsibilities with The Navigators.

Ruth, living with us for a time, fulfilled that role with me. Her heart, too, had been broken, and together we cried, embraced, reminisced, and prayed. Often, just a look between us would trigger tears, but they were healing, sympathizing, understanding tears that bound our hearts together in the terrible grief that had overtaken us. Marty often joined us for long talks, sharing memories and sorrow.

OUR NEED FOR SOLITUDE

Jerry and I felt the need to be apart, the need for solitude, as we began to put our lives back together. But we didn't want to leave our family and travel any distance away. Then, friends who had formerly lived in Colorado Springs and still maintained a home here called to offer that home to us as a daytime retreat, a place to reflect and rest and grieve in quiet and seclusion.

A few days after the funeral Jerry and I gathered our Bibles and a box full of sympathy cards and headed for the house. As we walked into that large, beautiful home, we felt a calm descend on our souls. Moving through the spacious, quiet rooms gave us a feeling of peace.

The house sat on a large lot surrounded by huge trees and bordered by tall lilac bushes, lushly blooming and fragrant in the warm spring air. The wonderful scent wafted through the open windows as we relaxed, prayed together, responded to the many cards and letters that had arrived, and began to talk together of our great loss.

For the first time in many days, we were alone. We could weep with abandon. We could lie down and rest undisturbed. We could think and talk and sorrow together.

With all of the loving support we had received from family and friends, we had very little time to talk together. We had watched the suffering of each other, but had not had time to express our sorrow or discuss it or even share the depth of loss we felt.

For several days, Jerry and I drove to the lovely house and spent the day there, sitting in quiet contemplation or walking the beautiful grounds, resting, writing in our journals, talking, weeping—always weeping.

We tried to put into words the depth of our feelings as we rested in that beautiful atmosphere. But the experience of restoration went beyond description. The beauty of the location and the welcome atmosphere of spring gave promise to a future springtime for our wounded souls.

SUBMITTING TO GRIEF'S PACE

Sleep continued to elude us. For a few nights following Steve's murder, I took sleeping pills but soon tried to rest naturally. That didn't happen. I would sleep deeply for a couple of hours and abruptly awaken, confused, disoriented. Then the reality of Steve's murder would settle over me like a cloud, and for an hour or more I would lie awake—grieving, praying, hurting.

Often I would notice by Jerry's breathing that he, too, was awake and grieving. My hand would steal toward his, or his toward mine, and we would lie in the dark, quietly talking of our great loss and our longings for Steve, tears dripping on our pillows. Our love for one another grew deep during those long, sleepless night hours as we shared our grief through tears and prayers and memories.

Steve was *our* son. Only Jerry could fully comprehend the depth of my sorrow, and I, Jerry's. Steve was a tangible evidence of our young love, our only son, a unique individual, a precious treasure to us. Even though we were convinced of his eternal, living soul, we had lost the possibility of communicating, touching, seeing him.

With no particular design or plan, merely feeling our way through the grief, Jerry and I were able to allow each other to grieve at our own pace. I cannot remember one time when Jerry suggested or even hinted to me that I should move from one phase of grief to the next, or that I was in some way delaying his own recovery.

We had no preparation or practice for such a critical blow to our individual emotional well-being, and to our marriage. Our love for each other and God's love for us provided a reservoir of strength to cope with our tragic plunge into grief. We deepened in our spiritual life and drew closer to one another than we had ever been in our marriage.

As we talked endlessly of Steve's death, we seldom used the word *murder*. The reality was still too fresh, too dreadful to confirm with that word. Instead we would say, "Steve died" or "Steve is gone" or "We lost Steve."

Dear God, what a strange term. Steve is truly lost to us. I feel like I'm searching for him. I'm always looking, but I can't find him. I know I won't find him in this lifetime, but my heart keeps searching. And my futile search hurts so much.

"Mary, he isn't lost. He's found. He's at home. He's peaceful and happy, more than you can imagine. Let your heart rest. Don't be troubled."

The pervading sorrow slowed and distracted my thinking processes. Consumed by grief, my thoughts were often irrational and illogical. When I tried to make decisions, think about current events, focus on necessary activities, or concentrate on conversations, my mind returned again and again to Steve's murder. I found it difficult to keep my thoughts focused for any length of time on anything but Steve's death.

I constantly thought about the night of Steve's death, the last few minutes of his life. Since the murderer had not been apprehended, we had no way of knowing the extent of what had happened in the cab that night.

The suffering he might have endured tormented my thoughts. My imagination conjured the most graphic and gruesome scenes possible. I knew it was fruitless speculation, but my agonized mind created terrible scenarios of the possible suffering Steve might have endured in the final moments of his life. Over and over and over again, I thought of Steve's last moments, my heart tormented by the injustice and cruelty of his death.

While I focused intensely on Steve's murder, I

fought against the idea that I was the mother of a murdered son. I didn't want that identity for a lifetime. I didn't want people to look at me and remember the murder of my son. I wanted my son back, living and whole, not ruthlessly murdered, forever gone. Intellectually I knew the longing was hopeless and irrational, but emotionally I yearned for the past when my family was intact.

Dear God, do I have to be the mother of a murdered son? I don't want that identity for the rest of my life. I want life to be as it was before. I want my family whole.

"Mary, think how terrible it would be to be a murderer's mother. At least your son was an innocent in this whole tragic affair. And remember, he is at peace. As much as you want him with you, he is enjoying something far better today."

WHEN A PARENT OUTLIVES A CHILD

I thought often about Steve dying before I did. Parents should model death for their children. Life takes on a peculiar distortion when a child dies first; something has gone dreadfully awry. All the plans and hopes a parent has dreamed for that loved child abruptly and painfully end. Contemplating the future without Steve brought endless waves of sorrow.

Again and again I thought, *God, I should have died first. I wanted to die first. There's something so wrong when a child dies first. I should have shown Steve how to die, modeled that for him. Now he's gone. He's gone.*

"Mary, death is painful either way. If you had died first, Steve would have suffered. Focus on your reunion

with him someday. And always remember, he is with Me. I love him far more than you do. He is safe, not suffering. He's happy, he's content, he's joyful."

I felt no motivation to resume normal life. The routine matters of daily living seemed a burden. Speaking, writing, study—those activities had been such a challenge. Now they seemed impossible as I struggled to concentrate, to think clearly, to organize.

I had always tried to practice self-discipline and, following my parents' example, tried to exhibit stoicism and strength. But the way my mind worked in those weeks and months following Steve's murder, I knew I was dealing with something beyond experience and self-discipline. No amount of personal resolve could force my mind into orderly, practical functioning. The shock, the sorrow, the terrible loss all combined to bring wreckage to the once organized processes of my mind.

Ironically, in the midst of all the pain, the fractured thinking, the irrationality, I sensed no personal fear. Fear simply didn't compute in the mass of intense emotions I felt every day. I had faced the worst thing God could ask of me, so what was there left to fear?

Chapter 9

FINDING COMFORT IN MEMORIES

My strong memories of those days are of falling tears. The smallest things would trigger weeping. A quick glance at a photograph of Steve . . . his favorite soft drink on the grocery shelf . . . a familiar song on the radio . . . another newspaper report on the murder investigation . . . a kind word from a friend . . . a sympathy card in the mail . . . Jerry's tears. Trying to control or halt my tears was a wasted exercise.

Dear God, am I destined to weep for the rest of my life? I can't imagine this terrible sorrow, this heaviness, this grinding pain ever going away. I get so tired of crying, Lord. I would like to stop crying for just one day.

"Mary, My dear, I see your tears. They are not *wasted. They show your love for Steve and the depth of your loss. Your tears will cleanse and heal your wounded spirit. Let them flow. Someday I'll wipe them all away. Someday you will laugh and rejoice and smile again."*

When the tears began to flow, I couldn't stop them. I didn't even try. The release was absolutely necessary. During casual conversations—in the grocery store, dining out with friends, driving the car— the tears flowed unchecked. I received curious stares from other people, but I could not restrain my tears.

Occasionally I would sob aloud. It was a reaction I couldn't anticipate and couldn't restrain. In public, at home, whether busy or quiet, the sob would come. It was not always accompanied by tears or even sad thoughts, but because I had cried so much, the reflex gasps continued.

I learned to carry a man's handkerchief. Paper tissues quickly lost their efficiency to absorb all the tears, and prolonged use irritated tender facial skin.

Women's fabric hankies were inadequate, but a man's handkerchief supplied "industrial size" capacity for tears, remained soft to the skin, and lasted for a good share of the day.

My appetite was slow in returning, and I rapidly lost weight. Good food is one of the pleasures of life, and I had lost my taste for pleasure. The taxing pressure of mourning narrowed my life to an all-consuming pain that didn't allow for pleasure. For many weeks friends continued to shower us with delicious prepared meals. Their kindness meant a great deal to me as I had little energy or interest in preparing meals for my family.

As the stress of grief continued, other physical symptoms surfaced. I developed mouth infections and sore throats. Jerry slowly acquired a deep hoarse cough and, ultimately, ulcers that needed treatment. We tried to guard our health as best we could, but the irrepressible grief slowly chipped away at our stamina and physical well-being.

PLEASE DON'T FORGET HIM

I felt an almost panicked desperation to keep Steve's memory alive. I dreaded the thought that people would forget him. I feared that people who loved him would be so repelled by his murder that they would want to forget, to put the tragedy behind them. I thought his life would be invalidated if anyone forgot him. I knew my feelings were irrational, but my deep love for Steve led me to anxiety about keeping his memory alive.

This apprehension led me to talk about Steve. I repeated again and again the story of his unjust murder, the continued search for his killer, and my loneliness for him. Friends and family kindly listened to my monologues. That gave me comfort. But inwardly I knew the value of Steve's life didn't depend on the memories of friends. Finally, a comforting thought invaded my grief.

It is enough that God remembers Steve. If everyone else forgets him, God will never forget. He does not forget those He loves. He will never forget. I can rest in that truth.

But, oh, how I missed him! I wanted so much to talk with him once again. One day a young man visiting in our home asked permission to call his mother in another state. For several minutes I listened to his part of the conversation as he laughed and talked to his mother, sharing ordinary, everyday events. I was overwhelmed with a sense of loss as I realized I would never have another conversation like that with Steve. I slipped away to another room to weep yet again.

Reminders of Steve's life brought sharp, searing pain that I tried to avoid. Every time I saw photos, clothes, familiar restaurants, streets, the radio station where he worked, or his friends, sharp sorrow reminded me of his absence. I tried to protect myself from that penetrating grief by avoiding places and things I usually associated with Steve.

EMBRACING MEMORIES OF STEVE

As I was encouraged to face the pain, to "lean" into it, I started to seek out memories of Steve's life. I knew I had to go *through* the grief instead of trying to *avoid* it. Gradually, I allowed memories to creep into my thoughts. I began to think about his babyhood, his growing years, his manhood.

I wanted to remember him as a contributing, caring, loving member of our family and society. Although each thought of Steve brought renewed pain, I began to appreciate memories of his life. Slowly I sought them out. Slowly I allowed myself to think about him—the joys, the struggles, the achievements.

As I inched my way into the memories of those happy days, I felt the warmth and joy and pride I had felt when Steve was a little boy. Although the memories were tinged with regrets and sadness, they gradually began to fill more of my thinking.

His birth brought so much joy to Jerry and me. We lived across the country from our immediate families and relied heavily on Jerry's grandmother. She was almost more excited about Steve's arrival than we were. After his birth she spent hours at the hospital watching him through the nursery window, commenting on his features, his size, his hair, longing for the moment she could hold him. The few weeks she spent with us following his birth gave us an example to follow after she left.

We were novices, as all new mothers and fathers are, and Steve bore the brunt of our early experimental attempts at parenting. We were much more tense and structured than we needed to be, carefully monitoring his food, his sleep habits, his growth. Steve seemed to weather our ineptitude quite well after he passed beyond his first few colicky months. As his colic lessened, and he gained more ability to entertain himself, his contentment increased.

He was a beautiful baby with silky blond hair, large hazel eyes, and incredibly long black eyelashes. I used to stand by his bassinet as he slept marveling over the perfection of his little face.

From infancy onward Steve was a reserved person. He met new people cautiously, watching silently before deciding if he should favor anyone with one of his slow, dazzling smiles. He was unusually satisfied with his own company. He could entertain himself for long periods of time with little books, and a few small toys or trinkets.

He loved to ride in the car and rarely made demands when the car was moving. Jerry spent his early career in the Air Force, which required several moves and lots of travel. Steve spent those long hours in the car quietly watching the passing scene or "reading" his little books. He was born before the advent of seat belts, and we made the entire back seat of the car into a little playground for him.

He displayed an early interest in learning. He would sit quietly while I read to him, worked puzzles with him, and tried to challenge his little mind with projects and activities. He liked to figure out things he didn't understand, working patiently to master complicated toys. He enjoyed engineering small designs by using anything at hand—sticks, boards, dirt, rocks.

Two years after his birth, he accepted the arrival of his first sister, Kathy, with equanimity. He rarely displayed jealousy and acknowledged her presence with big brother aplomb. He did the same when Karen arrived just as he was ready to begin kindergarten.

During those preschool years, Steve continued to show an interest in academic pursuits. I tried to provide as much stimulation as I could in spite of a busy schedule. He learned to read before he was three, absorbing simple books and sounding out words.

Sometimes when we were driving, he would watch

road signs, carefully and phonetically reading the words. He seemed to be in a hurry to learn all he could, as quickly as he could. He began to do simple arithmetic. I tried to help him understand the concepts using common items—vegetables, coins, dishes, little flash cards. Although I had never taught a preschool child, it seemed to me that Steve absorbed ideas and concepts easily.

An IQ test, requested by his first-grade teacher, confirmed his intellectual abilities. The results placed Steve in the genius category. Initially I was intimidated by the challenge of adequately stimulating and directing his intellectual capacity.

I soon realized that he was still a little boy with the need to play, to enjoy his friends, to dream, to lie on the grass and watch the clouds or the stars. He didn't need constant stimulus. His fertile mind provided that without continuous direction from me or Jerry or his teachers.

He did display some mischievous tendencies in his early school years. Fortunately, he had understanding teachers. In teacher-parent conferences, Jerry and I were told that he already knew most of the material being taught. He was bored much of the time. After he was given additional work to invigorate his interest, his contrary behavior diminished.

Reviewing the memories of Steve's childhood gradually brought warmth and comfort mingled with the everpresent pain of his absence.

NO LONGER BOUND BY TIME

As we moved through the first weeks following Steve's death, I felt an irrational need to mark the time he had been dead. Thursday always brought a fresh wave of pain.

"Steve has been gone for one week," I told Ruth, as we loaded the dishwasher one evening soon after the funeral. "Can it really be true? Maybe it's just a dream. Maybe I'll wake up and find Steve alive and well."

Ruth looked at me sadly, her sympathetic tears flowing with mine.

Again, that quiet inner voice reminded me of the real truth.

"Mary, remember that while each moment, each day, is filled with pain for you, your dear Steve has put time behind him. He lives in endless day. A thousand years with God are like a day that has just gone by. Your precious son knows time in a way you can only imagine. He is free, unbound by the rhythms of day and night, months, years. Time for him has no beginning, no end, no sorrow, no pressure. He is at peace."

Thank You, God. Just when I feel I cannot endure one more moment of this heavy, stifling sorrow, You give me a new perspective, a glimmer of hope.

I desperately wanted to see Steve again. His abrupt death had allowed no final farewell or loving gesture. I deeply regretted not being able to say good-bye. I felt if I could see him once, I would be satisfied. I couldn't shake this yearning to see him. I *longed* to see him just once more.

One night, when I was sleeping fairly peacefully, I dreamed of Steve. The scene was vivid. There was no background. The entire scene focused on Steve walking toward me wearing familiar clothes, smiling, relaxed. I moved toward him, reaching out to embrace him, and he faded from my sight as the dream ended.

The soothing yet graphic vision profoundly comforted me. I felt that God had allowed me to see Steve as he was, content, happy, peaceful. I never had another dream like that. I didn't need another. I had seen Steve.

A mirage? A hallucination? A wishful vision? I believe God allowed me to see Steve to satisfy the deep need of my broken mother's heart. I could rest after seeing his beloved face once more.

Chapter 10

MAKING PEACE WITH THE PAST

Mother's Day arrived two weeks after Steve's death. I faced the day with mounting apprehension. That special occasion brought a distinct reminder that my life as a mother had been forever changed.

The loss of all that defines the kinship between a mother and son produces a sorrow that lingers for a lifetime. There is an emptiness that never can be filled by another person. Healing comes, recovery slowly takes place, but the loneliness lasts for all time.

That first Mother's Day without Steve forced me to acknowledge that I had joined the sad assembly of mothers whose children have died.

In our work and travel, we meet many new people every year. A common question is, "Do you have children?"

As Mother's Day approached, I was troubled by the question, *"Do I have three children or four?"*

What will I tell people who ask about my family? If I say three, will that invalidate Steve's life? If I say four, will that be confusing? How do I explain Steve's terrible death? I can't introduce murder into a casual, introductory conversation. How many children do I have?

"Mary, of course you have four children. I am your God, I am Steve's God, whether you are living on earth or in Heaven. Steve is as much your son now as when he was alive on earth. You are linked forever by My love."

I learned to say "three" in some situations, and "four" in others. I found that it didn't matter as long as I knew *I* had four children.

Ruth, Julie, and our daughters planned a picnic for Mother's Day afternoon. We ate in a beautiful wooded area in the shadow of a huge rock. Photos of that day show some hesitant smiles as we inched through our first special family event without Steve.

At the end of lunch, Julie, knowing my love of plants, gave me a rose bush for my garden. Our daughters presented me with a mother's ring with my birthstone in the center and four stones representing our children's birth months circling the center stone.

As I opened the small package, Kathy said, "This is so you will remember that all of your children are equally close to your heart."

Of course the tears flowed once more, but now the tears were ones of appreciation and love, as well as sorrow.

Later that day a friend called from California. One of her adult sons had died in a river rafting accident several years before. She had traveled the path of sorrow I now walked.

Sobbing, I asked her, "How long does this pain last? Will I hurt like this forever?"

"Mary, shock is controlling you right now," she replied. "You are in extreme sorrow. Time will remove some of the pain you now feel. Allow yourself to think about Steve. Remember the good times, even though it brings pain. It will help you."

"But I can't even bear to look at his picture. It's too painful. Will I ever be able to think of him again without pain?"

"Mary, I still miss my son very much, but I no longer grieve. Be patient. God will comfort and heal you, but give it time."

Oh God, maybe the day will come for me, too, when I no longer grieve. Maybe this pain will ease at some point in the future. I think I could stand to miss Steve if only this terrible pain would ease.

Her mother's heart, broken like mine, reached out to give me hope that time and God's love do heal wounds too deep to describe. She encouraged me to keep reading the Bible, to pray, and to find a loving friend who would pray with me.

Fortunately, Ruth remained in the States for several months, living with us, and she endlessly listened and prayed and encouraged. She generously shared my grief, listening patiently as I repeated my sorrow and bewilderment over Steve's murder.

Taking my friend's advice, I allowed more memories to flow on Mother's Day. I thought back on Steve's growing years.

HURTLING TOWARD MANHOOD

Steve spent six of his elementary school years on the Air Force Academy where we lived while Jerry was a professor of astronautics. Steve loved the wooded land surrounding our housing area, and the tight-knit community provided a safe environment for children to play in this natural setting. Weather was no deterrent; children played together in the snow of winter and the searing high country sunshine of summer.

Following Jerry's resignation from the Air Force, we moved into Colorado Springs where Steve began attending a small private school. He excelled academically without much effort—a fact that troubled us as we felt he might be wasting some of his intellectual potential.

For a few semesters he attended early morning advanced math classes at the local public high school, then jumped on his bike and pedaled furiously to arrive at his school in time for the first class there.

Those additional classes seemed to help him direct his academic energies.

Although Steve had been exceptionally long at birth — twenty-two-and-a-half inches — his growth pattern was slow. He remained small through his elementary school years.

Then, during his freshman and sophomore years in high school, he grew twelve inches to a height of six feet. He suddenly discovered the social and athletic life that had been denied him because of his small, bookish appearance. He took advantage of the changes to enter a world he had not known before.

Jerry and I were concerned about his sudden academic indifference. We had little hard evidence, as he still received top grades, but we were dealing with a new and independent person. Perhaps all parents feel as we did — somewhat baffled — realizing we were relating with a near adult capable of and eager to make his own decisions while we wanted to maintain certain restraints. Although Steve didn't *rebel* in the classic sense of leaving home and living a debauched life, we did have some heated discussions about his activities and choices.

I feel Jerry and I were unnecessarily concerned about Steve's future. He had always shown an exceptional amount of dependability and good judgment. But he was the hapless recipient of our experimental parenting. We were trying to decide how directive we should be and how much we should release him to his own judgment and decisions. We had never dealt with a teenager before, and we were feeling our way, just as he was striving for manhood.

He was financially responsible and didn't demand much from Jerry and me. He maintained a savings account that he designated for college use. He developed a small business re-covering worn Bibles with new leather. He didn't make a lot of money but carefully used what he had. After his death, many people wrote to remind us that Steve had re-covered their Bibles and those Bibles were still in use many years later.

Looking back, I think those were happy years for Steve. He was busy with church activities, school sports, music participation. He had excellent male role models. Two in particular, a teacher and a church leader, encouraged him by instilling spiritual values and strong ethics in his life. They also gave him wonderful practical experiences.

His science teacher, Darrel Valdois, taught him to rock climb, a sport Steve loved. Darrel instructed a group of students as they learned to rappel and observe stringent safety measures while climbing high above the ground.

Bob Nass, leader of a young men's organization in our church, gave him experience in mountain camping, even snow camping, which Steve declared great fun!

He loved outdoor activity and eagerly participated in hiking, camping, and fishing. He learned to fish with his hands, standing patiently in the icy streams of the Colorado mountains, waiting to snatch an unsuspecting trout with his hands as it swam lazily by. If it was outdoors, active, and adventurous, Steve liked it.

He never developed an interest in hunting. Although when visiting his great-grandmother's farm one summer, he used her rifle to shoot frogs in the pond behind the barn. He prevailed on Grandma to fry the frog legs. They both declared the result delicious.

For several years he attended a youth camp, Eagle

Lake, in the mountains above Colorado Springs. Combining vigorous outdoor activity with spiritual training and lots of fun, Eagle Lake gave Steve a yearly experience that built his spiritual life, self-esteem, and wilderness skills. He attended as long as he was age-eligible.

FORESHADOW OF A FUTURE SEPARATION

In spite of his casual attitude toward his studies, he graduated as valedictorian of his small high school. Just as Steve completed high school, Jerry was asked to move to Seattle to supervise Navigator staff in the western region of the United States. Steve chose to remain in Colorado Springs and attend university there.

I felt as though part of my heart had been ripped out as we drove away leaving him behind. Does every mother feel that way as she separates from her firstborn?

Many times on this first Mother's Day without Steve, I thought of a conversation he and I had six months earlier. We drove to Iowa together to see relatives. Because of his work schedule and my Navigator commitments, we made a very quick trip. We drove through the night to get there, stayed for only a brief time, and then drove straight back. We had made this trip before to see his great-grandmother, and found that we thoroughly enjoyed each other's company.

During those long hours in the car, we had some wonderful talks. Nearing home on that trip, Steve suddenly said, "Mom, I don't think I'm going to live to be very old. I think I'm going to die young."

I felt my breath catch. My heart began to pound. "Steve, what makes you say that?"

There was a long pause. Finally, he said, "I just have this strong feeling that I won't live to be very old."

"Oh, honey, only God knows the time of our death. We can't possibly know when we're going to die. You're a young man. You likely have many years to live."

I paused. "Please don't die before I do. I couldn't bear to lose you."

He didn't elaborate on his shocking opinion. I had no idea what else to say. I felt dread settle over me, and drove in silence for many miles.

I was stunned by his comments. Steve frequently had intuitions or forewarnings of events that were about to happen. Could his comments to me have been an indication that God was preparing him for the future and, indirectly, preparing me?

In the next few months I thought many, many times of Steve's comments. I didn't even tell Jerry of our conversation. Steve and I never talked of it again. Perhaps I avoided mentioning it because of the ominous tone of his statement. When I heard that he had been murdered, his prediction immediately returned to my mind.

Steve, my dear, how often did you think about your own death? Were you frightened? I wish we had talked about it again. You seemed so casual when you spoke with me about it. Were you at peace? I know you're at peace now. But, oh, how very much I miss you. I dread all of the Mother's Days in the future without you. I love you . . . I love you.

WHAT MIGHT HAVE BEEN

I found that if I thought of Steve's childhood for just a short while, I could bear it, and the comfort of remembering the good days of his childhood helped relieve my agonizing sorrow.

As I allowed the happy memories of Steve's childhood to wash through my tortured mind, I found solace in remembering the pride and joy I felt when he was a boy. Jerry and I talked often of Steve's childhood. Together we tried to resurrect as many memories as we could. Even as we thought of the happy times, we felt the sting of regret that we hadn't created even more memories to comfort us in our terrible loss.

Jerry, especially, struggled with regrets.

"I wish we had gone fishing more often. . . . Maybe I should have urged him to attend a different college. . . . I regret that I didn't play more tennis with him. . . . Should I have persuaded him to quit his taxi work?"

"Jerry, dear," I encouraged him, "remember the good times. Don't torment yourself with memories of what might have been. You loved Steve with all of your heart. You are a wonderful, caring father. You were the best father you knew how to be for Steve."

Although Jerry's regrets were understandable, they didn't help in his grief healing until he realized they were longings to be with Steve rather than authentic memories of past failings. Gradually his regrets eased, and he was able to view his life as a father with a more realistic perspective and confidence.

Jerry later wrote:

Do we have regrets? Yes. There are many things we wish we had done. More time with Steve. We always think there will be more time, but for us there wasn't. We wish we had urged him to quit driving the taxi. Yet these regrets cannot redo the past. We cannot live with regrets. We tried to do the best we knew to do—and in our rational moments we are at peace with the past.

Chapter 11

STRUGGLING WITH THE PRESENT

For some reason, the death of a sibling doesn't strike much sympathy or understanding among many people. It seems to be regarded as the least traumatic of family losses.

One of our daughters was approached by an acquaintance six weeks after Steve's funeral.

"Well, are you over it yet?"

"No, of course not."

"But he was *just* your brother."

Stunned, our daughter couldn't answer. She turned away, her heart broken by this unintentionally cruel remark.

With or without full understanding and sympathy from their friends, our daughters had to walk through the sorrow and loss. I ached to see their grief. Kathy and Karen had their husbands to share their grief, but Kristie often mentioned that she had to guard her expressions of grief because most of her friends couldn't comprehend the depth of her loss.

The reality is that losing a brother or sister devastates the siblings left behind. The comfortable, familiar family structure has broken. Those remaining wonder what family life would have been like in ten or twenty or forty years. Every family gathering will always be a reminder of the one who isn't there.

Doubts and questions may bother remaining siblings. Does Mom wish it had been me? How can I make up for my brother's death? Should I, in some way, try to fulfill *his* dreams? Why can't people understand how painful this is for me?

As I watched them struggle, a heaviness for my daughters' sorrow weighed on me. Jerry and I searched for books or tapes addressing sibling loss, but found little. Finally I invited two women whose siblings had died as young adults to come for an afternoon luncheon and talk with our daughters. Their understanding and empathy gave our daughters a sympathetic place to express all they had been feeling since the murder of their brother.

One evening, when I had resumed watching the television news, an update on the search for Steve's killer came on the screen. A picture of a tow truck hauling Steve's cab from the scene flashed into view. Then a close-up of the interior of the cab complete with wide, dark stains on the upholstery appeared on the screen. I recoiled from the terrible sight.

My darling Steve, that's your blood staining the cab. Oh, how terrible. . . . My dear . . . my dear. . . . I should have been with you. I would have died for you. It's so wrong. So unfair. What a great wickedness against you. I'm so sorry, my dear Steve. I love you. I wish I could have died for you.

Ruth immediately shut off the TV, but the images remained, vivid, graphic, terrible. I wrapped my arms around myself, tears streaming down my face. Ruth came over to hug me. The horrible pictures I had seen drove home the reality of Steve's brutal death. Terrible as it was, I knew I needed to accept the stark, painful truth of it.

When a friend first mentioned, the day following the murder, the police efforts to catch the killer, I shrank from the idea.

"I hope they never catch him," I responded. "I couldn't bear to look at him. What kind of horrible person could blast away the back of Steve's head and leave him crumpled, dead, in his cab? I never, never want to see that person. I couldn't stand it!"

"Mary, dear, do you want that person running

loose, perhaps harming someone else?"

The thought struck me like a hammer blow.

Dear God, of course not. If the murderer isn't caught, some other mother might have to feel this harrowing grief. Please help the police, the detectives, everyone who is trying to find the killer. Don't let him kill again.

A CRASH COURSE IN THE LAW

We found ourselves in an alien world. My brush with the law to this point had been a couple of parking violations. Suddenly I was dealing with the most horrifying of violent crimes. We quickly learned the intricacies of law enforcement, crime investigation, and defendants' rights.

Steve was referred to as the "victim." There were times when I wanted to cry, "*Wait. Wait a minute. This is my precious son you're talking about. He has a name. He's dead, murdered. Doesn't his life count? Where is justice?*"

As our family stumbled through the early days of grief, the police continued doggedly, carefully searching for clues that would lead to Steve's killer. Evidence was distressingly scarce.

Steve's wallet remained in his pocket, so robbery didn't seem likely. He carried a bag with change for fares, but it was untouched. Earlier in the day he had deposited money in his bank and was carrying very little with him. If not robbery, then what?

The cab company tape recorded all requests for cabs. The police used the recording of the call Steve answered. With the cooperation of radio stations in Colorado, the recording was played several times, along with the request that anyone recognizing the voice call local authorities.

Of the people who responded, several, including a parole officer, were sure the voice belonged to a man who was currently on probation. The police located the identified suspect. The man was a known felon in the area.

The police found evidence that he had purchased a gun a few days before Steve's murder, but they were unable to locate the weapon. Because he was a convicted felon, he was arrested for purchasing a gun. A judge ordered him held in custody until he gave a voice sample for analysis and comparison with the voice on the cab company recording.

The investigators continued at a diligent pace, searching for any further clues.

Although the police kept us abreast of the investigation and the apprehension of the suspect, the process remained abstract in my mind until the first time I saw a photo of the suspect in the newspaper. A terrible weight settled over my heart.

Was this the last face Steve saw before he died? It isn't right. It isn't fair. Was the murderer's face angry, vicious, taunting? Did Steve feel fear, despair, horror? He should have seen a loving, cherished face in his last moments. Why did it have to be that face?

"Mary, I was there in his last moments. And the first face he saw after he died was Mine. You don't need to worry about those last moments. I know all about them. Think about your son now—happy, serene, content, rejoicing."

I was often drawn back to that newspaper clipping to look at the suspect's face and wonder if he was truly guilty. I speculated over and over what his and

Steve's last words might have been. Why didn't Steve make any attempt to save himself? What prevented him from rolling out of the cab, running away, fighting for his life? No sign of a struggle existed in the scant evidence remaining.

Instead, only bullet holes in the windshield, one bullet and bullet fragments remained behind. Although Steve's cab was painstakingly searched for clues, few surfaced. Only a partial fingerprint remained on one door handle to offer a small clue.

I learned to wait patiently for the next small development in the search for clues. We heard often from the detectives, and that made the waiting easier.

STRUGGLING BACK TOWARD "NORMAL"

As the sorrow and pain continued, and my emotions remained fragile, I wanted to stay at home, hiding. I felt comfortable among family and close friends but shied away from the stares and speculation of crowds. However, I couldn't hide. That wasn't possible. If I had lived in the nineteenth century, I would have donned black clothing and remained in seclusion for a year. Our culture doesn't allow for that luxury.

I had to mingle once again. Our family had to take up familiar schedules again. Jerry resumed his responsibilities with The Navigators. Julie returned to her classroom. Kristie went back to college.

As we were thrust into public occasions once more, we attended many events that reminded us that Steve wasn't there to share them with us.

Shortly after the funeral, my nephew Danny competed in a large high school track meet. For the first time since the funeral, I was in public. The entire family attended together, cheering for our favorite athlete.

I felt shattered inside, shrinking from the boisterous excitement around me even while enthusiastically applauding Danny's efforts. For the first time in my life I knew the true meaning of *mixed emotions*. A verse from Proverbs slipped into my mind.

Even in laughter the heart may ache, and joy may end in grief (Proverbs 14:13).

As we sat in the stands for several hours in the warm Colorado sunshine, watching healthy young men and women competing on the field, my mind kept drifting to thoughts of Steve, still young, now buried in a nearby cemetery, his strong legs forever stilled, his competitive spirit forever silenced by a murderer's bullets.

Even as I cheered, I huddled between Jerry and Kristie, wanting to avoid attention. I knew many of the people at the track meet, and they knew of Steve's murder. I dreaded people looking at me and thinking of the murder.

Danny contended valiantly for a win, and in his final competition of the day, he gave a bold effort that resulted in a winner's ribbon. He presented it to me with a hug, telling me it was "in memory of Steve." Of course the tears flowed again as I received that generous token of Danny's loving concern for me and warm memories of his dead cousin.

Travel was a frequent aspect of Jerry's work. Travel demands forced a decision shortly after Steve's death. For nearly five years, Jerry had been helping to plan a conference for world-wide leadership in The Navigators. Forty countries would be represented. The meeting held significance for planning, interaction, fellowship, and motivation.

Due to financial considerations, spouses were not included at this meeting, but with counsel from Doug Sparks, who had been so helpful to us the day we learned of Steve's murder, we decided I should go.

"This is not the time for you to be apart," Doug said. "You need each other now."

The meeting convened in the beautiful hills of the island country of Cypress. The local director of the conference brought his wife so that I would have a companion during the meeting times. I had known Marilyn for many years. Now she spent hours with me, strolling through the lanes of the mountainside retreat, listening to my story of grief, adding her tears to mine as we talked of the great sorrow in losing a child.

One evening Jerry and I told the assembled leadership about Steve's murder. We shared our continuing sorrow and our deep appreciation for their prayers and condolences. All of them had faxed or called at the time of Steve's death. Many had done so more than once. As we related the events of recent weeks, I broke down several times and could not speak. Jerry continued when I began to weep.

The concern of our international colleagues touched me deeply. They allowed us to relate the terrible news and responded with assurances of their continued prayers for us.

During that trip we tried to protect our health, knowing from experience the physical toll exacted by international travel. We had been warned to drink only pure water, so I was careful to use the water provided in a carafe in our room. One day I was in our room as the maid arrived to tidy up. I watched with astonishment, and then amusement, as she took the carafe to the bathroom and filled it from the tap!

We returned home in time for my niece's wedding shortly after her graduation from college. Steve's death could have cast a melancholy atmosphere over the festivities. We determined that would not happen.

When I first took Susie into my arms after learning of Steve's murder, I told her, "Susie, this does not change our joy for you. We will have a wonderful celebration on June 10. Don't let this rob you of the happiness God intends for you. Steve would want you to have a joyous, happy wedding day."

And a great wedding it was, with much love and celebration. There was a special intensity and sense of togetherness in the family, made more acute by Steve's absence. Susie had asked Steve to man the video camera, and his absence was marked for me as I watched someone else perform that task. Again, during that beautiful ceremony, I felt the dichotomy of warm happiness with the underlying layer of deep sorrow.

As we struggled to return to normal, "firsts" remained difficult. Any time we did something for the first time following Steve's murder, I felt the sting of his absence.

Church attendance had always held a special attraction for me. I enjoyed the music, the sermons, the atmosphere of worship and praise. But several Sundays went by before I could bring myself to sit in the church auditorium where Steve's memorial service had been held. Jerry didn't seem to feel the same resurgence of memories that I did, and often he went without me.

111

The memories were so strong, the pain so acute, that I shrank from entering the sanctuary. As much as I wanted to attend the services, I allowed myself to remain in a more comfortable place. We continued to attend our Sunday class where the love and understanding and sympathy were palpable.

Finally I resumed church attendance, huddling in the rear of the auditorium, weeping silently during beautiful music presentations or especially touching messages. Gradually the benefits outweighed the pain of the memories there, and I resumed regular attendance.

Stacks of mail continued to arrive. Friends, colleagues, family, even strangers from all over the world continued to write; some wrote many times. They all wanted to express their sympathy for us, their sorrow at Steve's murder, their assurances of prayers. One friend wrote weekly for some time, sending cards, letters, encouraging notes, little gifts. The postman couldn't stuff all the mail into our mailbox and came daily to the door with bundles of letters.

Julie, too, received many, many letters. Her postman said, "What's going on here? A wedding?"

Julie answered, "I only wish it were a wedding. We have had a funeral."

I welcomed each letter. I avidly read every printed poem, each generic expression of condolence, and most especially the personal notes of sympathy.

All of them expressed condolences to us, but many of them also included remembrances of Steve, incidents from his childhood, photographs, memories of special help he had provided with his taxi service, his rescue of a family in a burning home, and more. I treasured these letters, reading them, and an hour later taking them out to read again as tears streamed down my face.

Many of them told of the loss of their own children. Others told us that they had lost loved ones through homicide. In sorrow and concern they reached out to offer encouragement that the pain would heal.

Excerpts from those letters communicate the deep concern and compassion that flowed our way during those days.

My heart breaks for you whenever I think of Steve's murder. I don't know how you have been able to bear it. My thoughts are with you day and night.

There is so little one can say that would be of any help or comfort . . . but we can always pray.

It's hard to watch folks we love and appreciate go through times of sorrow. Because we love you, we hold you up in prayer. God bless and comfort you.

You don't know me, but I attended the conference in Columbus, Ohio, when the announcement of your son's murder was made. I just wanted you to know that I'm praying for you and your family. There's a line in "Fairest Lord Jesus" that makes me think of you. It says, "Jesus is purer, who makes the woeful heart to sing."

We were so sorry to hear of the loss of your dear son, Steve. As parents of an only son, our hearts ache for you. Our love and prayers are with you.

We lost our youngest son to leukemia seven years ago in May. I believe God really wants me to say to you that it will get better. The pain you feel now, that weight that you feel on your shoulders will ease in time.

I think of you with misty vision and aching heart. It seems incredible that one such terrible act by one sinner should rob so many people of such an irreplaceable treasure. I couldn't count the number of times we've thought and talked of you, and upon remembrance of you, we've prayed for you.

Wonderful letters, concerned letters continued to flow to our home for weeks and months. In our deep fatigue, answering each letter individually presented a daunting task. We keenly appreciated the outpouring of concern for us and felt a desire and need to respond. Finally we decided to write a long letter, which we printed in bulk and sent to each one who had written, faxed, or sent telegrams. An excerpt from that seven-page letter reveals our still stark grief.

This is a long letter. Perhaps it is more a need for us to write it than for you to read it. Thanks for bearing with us. How do you describe thirty years of life in a few pages? How do you communicate the sense of loss and grief that we feel today? Words seem so inadequate. We are slowly coming to grips with the reality of his death. But daily we are confronted with the "nevers" of the future. Steve will never again walk in and say "Hi Mom, Hi Dad." He will never do his radio show on KRCC again. He will never be the "Santa Claus" at Christmas gift openings around our tree. He will never play with his nephews again. The list is endless and painful . . . so what now? We must go on with our lives. Steve would have wanted it no differently. Although we miss him terribly, we know with a certainty that life does not end with death and we have much to live for. We have children, grandchildren, and Julie to think of and to care for. We focus our hope and confidence in God as we experience His help, comfort, and healing. . . . Thank you for your many expressions of sympathy and love to us.

Chapter 12

STUMBLING THROUGH THE FIRST YEAR

In the following months, we saw many people we hadn't seen since before Steve's death. With each meeting we repeated the painful process of sharing the details of the murder, our mourning, our emotions, and the search for the murderer. Every repetition brought the ache of grief to the forefront again, but also gave vent to our pent-up emotions. We continued to be amazed at the caring and concern of so many friends and colleagues.

We realized the depth of care that existed for us when we talked with an acquaintance at a wedding reception.

He said, "I am so sorry for your loss. I have felt so keenly the pain you must feel. The other day I was driving to an appointment when I felt overwhelmed by Steve's murder. I pulled to the side of the road, crying, and prayed that God would let me carry your pain for the rest of the day. I wanted you to have some relief."

We were amazed by the depth of sorrow this man shared with us. Of course his concern and sympathy brought tears in that atmosphere of celebration. But it brought a sense of deep comfort as well.

Everywhere, we found that people wanted to help us, to grieve with us, to make some gesture in memory of Steve. The school where Julie taught fifth grade planted a tree in the front lawn as a memorial to Steve. In a little ceremony remembering him, the beautiful token of remembrance was placed in the ground.

My brothers and sisters, in town for Susie's wedding six weeks following Steve's death, planted three beautiful quaking aspen in our back yard in memory of Steve. The trees' vivid color in the fall brought a bright spot of encouragement and remembrance. As I viewed them, I could visualize Steve hiking in the high country during the crisp fall season when the mountain aspen were at their golden best.

As special occasions came—birthdays, anniversaries, reunions—we were reminded anew of Steve's absence. Beginning with Ruth's birthday on Steve's burial day, and moving through many other family occasions, we faced those "firsts" with aching hearts and heavy thoughts.

Jerry's birthday in June brought memories of the previous year; Steve was the only family member available to celebrate with a planned mountain picnic. The day was chilly and drizzly, damp and miserable to the point we almost canceled the trip to the mountains.

But Steve, always invigorated by adverse conditions, said, "Come on, let's go! What's a little rain?"

Bundled in winter coats, we ate our picnic huddled in a shelter near a small mountain lake. Our talk that day turned to spiritual matters.

A SPIRITUAL LEAP

Jerry and I strongly felt the significance of spiritual training for our children as they were growing up. We prayed that they would develop deep spiritual values. We wanted each of our children to learn early in life of the nature of God, the love of Jesus, the value of the Bible, and the reality of prayer. Every day we spent time with our children reading the Bible, discussing beliefs and values, praying together.

We wanted a spiritual life for our children that moved beyond an academic exercise to an enjoyable and practical relevance of faith in daily life. Steve participated in many discussions and family conversations regarding values and spiritual concepts. Often he would offer helpful insights punctuated with his wry humor.

We found cause for concern as he entered university. He lived with friends during his first year of university, then moved into a place of his own. Those were transitional years for Steve as he struggled toward full independence—spiritual, financial, and emotional. He endeavored to reconcile the spiritual teachings of childhood with the teachings in his university classes.

His childhood faith faltered and began to deteriorate. But even during his struggles he lived his Christian values, and at one point said, "I live by my parents' principles."

Watching from a distance, Jerry and I prayed and wavered between hope and discouragement. Even as we watched his spiritual conflict, we saw a rising conviction and compassion and concern toward the poor, the disenfranchised, the downtrodden, the victims of injustice. He developed a keen social conscience that was reflected in his help toward the poor and needy.

Shortly before his marriage and graduation from university, we returned to Colorado Springs to live. We watched Steve seek his place in life. He was not motivated by a desire for material things. He was perfectly happy with a simple lifestyle. Status, money, and prestige held no attraction for him.

That attitude determined his career choices. His education would have afforded higher paying jobs than he chose, but he preferred to stay with jobs in which he was comfortable and found personal satisfaction. He worked for a travel agency, conducted a radio show, and purchased and drove his own cab.

It was with his cab driving that he tried to serve people. He had steady customers among the blind, the aged, the infirm, the lonely, and the poor. He would assist them from their homes, into doctors' offices, by carrying their parcels. In short, going beyond mere transportation to caring assistance.

As we talked that cold, misty day in the mountains, Steve said, "Mom and Dad, I'm taking the leap of faith back to God."

The next months before his death brought many opportunities to talk about his feelings and thoughts and spiritual renewal. I will always be grateful for those talks.

REMEMBERING STEVE AND JULIE TOGETHER

Steve and Julie's wedding anniversary evoked so much emotion. It was difficult to remember their lovely wedding day, to know that Julie was now alone, a young widow, Steve forever gone.

Julie and Steve chose an outdoor setting for their wedding on the grounds of a beautiful estate, the former home of the founder of Colorado Springs. Colorado weather is unpredictable, fluctuating between balmy and frigid. The day of their wedding dawned sunny and warm.

Guests sat in the shade of tall pine trees dwarfed by the towering rocks overhead. Mountain blue jays flitted among the treetops as Steve and Julie pledged their vows to one another.

Julie is artistic and creative. The wedding confirmed that as she came with her bridesmaids to that lovely setting, dressed in beautiful gowns she had designed and made. The reception was held on the sweeping lawns of the estate in the warmth and sunshine of that picture-perfect day.

Steve and Julie would have no more anniversaries. The celebrations were stilled forever, cut off by a murderer's bullets.

Never again would I see Steve in the home where he and Julie lived near the downtown area. His neighborhood was racially, economically, and generationally mixed. He liked that.

In discussing the differences between our neighborhoods, he told me, "Mom, I live with a genuine mix of people. In your neighborhood, they're all clones!"

He chose a different political perspective from ours and often talked about his reasons for thinking as he did. I was stimulated by our talks. I found that he based his political views on a deep concern for people. Even though I couldn't agree with all of his convictions, we often had invigorating discussions without rancor. I took heart from his obvious concern for the needs and suffering of people.

The years between our return to Colorado Springs and Steve's murder were gratifying to me as I was able to see Steve more often after the geographical separation of five years. After Steve's marriage to Julie, we saw them quite often, although they were busy and our visits were often spontaneous and unplanned.

They loved all mountain activity—camping, cross-country skiing, hiking—always with their Afghan hounds running alongside. Those outdoor adventures were gone forever.

For weeks Julie, Jerry, and I delayed selecting a headstone for Steve's grave. Finally we made an appointment. As we wandered among the marble stones, I wondered how much sadness had come into that place. Julie selected a beautiful black marble stone, one that would have pleased Steve. Together we designed the text and artwork.

When it was in place, I looked at it often on my visits to the cemetery. The permanence of that solid square of marble reminded me of God's unchanging love. The mountain scene etched into it provided a reminder of Steve's love of nature, the beauty that surrounded us in spite of the inner turmoil of our souls.

I visited the cemetery more often than other family members. We were learning that each of us needed to grieve in individual ways. I was comforted by a trip to the cemetery, sitting alone in that beautiful place, remembering Steve, praying, often leaning against the headstone. I found solace in the quiet grandeur of that mountain valley. Other family members found the reminders there too painful and preferred to think of and grieve for Steve in more familiar settings.

I often found flowers lying near Steve's headstone, a consoling reminder that he had not been forgotten.

THE NEVER AGAINS

There were still painful days ahead. Steve's birthday brought excruciating memories. I couldn't seem to fight back thoughts of bygone birthdays. And finally, thinking of the suggestion to move *through* the grief instead of trying to go around it, I let the memories flow.

His first birthday in Florida, as he cautiously watched the single flaming candle and then dug unreservedly with his hands into the chocolate frosting, smearing it liberally across his little face. His fourth birthday when he celebrated with a breakfast with

Santa Claus shared with his great-grandmother and his special friend Barbara. His seventh birthday when he fought back the effects of stomach flu long enough to enter the living room and unwrap the long desired bicycle before stumbling back to bed. His thirteenth birthday as he proudly proclaimed his entrance into his long-awaited teens . . . his eighteenth birthday when he registered to vote . . . his thirtieth and final birthday . . . his thirty-first birthday, which he would never experience.

The memories flooded in, joyful, funny, sad, and poignant. I looked at pictures. I prayed. I cried. I spent the day weeping and remembering and longing.

Dear God, this is his first birthday in Heaven. It's not right. It's not fair. Where is justice? He should be here where I could give him a hug and wish him a happy birthday and give him a gift, take him and Julie to dinner. I can't bear it that he's dead, never to have another birthday . . . never another day to live and laugh and love. Please tell him today how much I love him.

And, then, finally, at the end of that long, painful day, a comforting thought began to emerge and predominate in my tortured thinking.

We did have him for thirty birthdays . . . thirty happy, wonderful birthdays to file away in our memory banks and bring out and savor for a long time to come. Thank You, God, for those thirty years.

But, please, please, help us through each day. It is so painful to think about the "never-agains." I'll never again buy a card that says, "Happy Birthday, Son." The only gift I give him now is flowers for his grave. I'll never again celebrate with him. I'll never see him reach his thirty-fifth birthday, or his fortieth, or any other birthday. But thank You for the thirty birthdays we did have. Help me to be grateful.

Steve's birthday fell just before Christmas. Thinking that we would be comforted by following traditions, we carried on with Christmas as we had known it for years. Family gathered at our home, gifts were exchanged, carols sung, familiar traditions observed. Instead of comfort, I felt an overwhelming sense of loss and desolation. Family members treated me with care and concern, but the emptiness left by Steve's absence was too huge a void to be filled with familiar activities.

On the surface I rejoiced over Christ's advent, thanked loved ones for gifts, cooked traditional foods, laughed and sang at the right times. Inwardly my emotions were leaden, and ahead of me I saw years and years of holiday celebrations without the presence of Steve.

I kept thinking back to the previous Christmas when Steve sat on the floor near me following our traditional dinner and quickly composed a poem about the bland flavor, strong odor, and jellylike consistency of lutefisk, a traditional Norwegian fish often prepared for Christmas gatherings. He read his hastily created poem to the assembled family amid much laughter and agreement.

O LUTEFISK
Languishing lonely on my plate
Everything else I already ate.
Quivering pile so clear and so near,
Please—can't I wash it down with just one more beer?
They say Vikings carried the stuff on their ships
But guaranteed, had they had anything else,

125

It would never have touched their lips.
Cod-soaked lye sitting in front of me,
Come on now, think—I need a strategy
Oops—it slid right off my plate.
Eat it, Caesar, you canine ingrate.
What? "No, Mom," I say, "I don't want any more,"
As I grind helping number one into the floor.
Tradition!

I knew how much I would miss his presence in years to come, how I would miss his unusual and personal creative gifts, his help in the kitchen, his enjoyment of his nephews, his warmth and wit.

We learned that first Christmas that traditions are fine. They should continue, most of them, at least, but we needed to add new traditions and activities that did not carry the weight of memories, that allowed us to define our family by the new look that came when Steve no longer joined special celebrations.

Someone sent me a poem that gave me courage and hope as I faced that first Christmas without Steve. I read it many times that Christmas season, and the tears always flowed, but it helped me to visualize Steve's present reality.

I've had my first Christmas in heaven,
a glorious wonderful day.
I stood with the saints of the ages
Who found Christ the Truth and the Way;
I sang with the heavenly choir;
Just think! I who so loved to sing!
And Oh, what celestial music
We brought to our Savior and King.
We sang the glad songs of redemption,

How Jesus to Bethlehem came,
And how they called His name "Jesus,"
That all might be saved by His Name.
We sang once again with the angels,
The song that they sang that blest morn,
When shepherds first heard the glad story
That Jesus the Savior was born.
Oh, dear ones, I wish you had been here,
No Christmas on earth can compare,
With all of the raptures in heaven,
The songs of the angels so fair.
You know how I always loved Christmas
It seemed such a wonderful day
With all of my loved ones around me
The children so happy and gay.
Yes, now I can see why I loved it.
And Oh, what a joy it will be
When you, all my loved ones are with me
To share in the glories I see.
So, dear ones on earth, here's my greeting:
"Look up till the Day Star appears,
And Oh, what a Christmas awaits us,
Beyond all the parting and tears."

—Unknown

We ignored New Year's celebrations that year, partly from emotional fatigue, and also from an apathy toward celebration of any kind. We did feel a glimpse of hope that the powerful pangs of grief were beginning to recede. It hurt to realize that 1991 would be the first year Steve would not be with us. Our first full year as a fractured family.

127

Chapter 13

CLOSURE AT LAST

One by one we passed milestones and finalized the fallout from Steve's death.

Activity that had once been commonplace but set aside during the sharp days of mourning became commonplace once again. Jerry's travel schedule increased. My responsibilities couldn't be neglected any longer. We found some consolation in returning to the normal activity of life.

The district attorney called us to his office several times to receive briefings from the police on the latest developments in the case. These sessions were graphic and painful as they described the murder scene in detail. At the same time, I was comforted as I realized the police were moving closer to solving Steve's murder.

We learned that every procedure moved at a snail's pace. I discovered two reasons for the sluggish pace of justice. One is the absolute consideration given to the rights of the accused. Our entire justice system is based on the premise of innocent until proven guilty. Painstaking care is given to each small detail in the investigation to be certain errors don't occur that result in the conviction of an innocent person. Conversely, the same care is taken not to release a guilty felon.

The second reason is the overwhelming number of criminal cases that jam our courts. It is almost impossible for the system to keep up with the heavy flow of cases while giving fair attention to the accused.

For families of the victims, this logjam in the justice system brings great frustration. Each family of a murder victim feels keenly the need to see justice quickly and fairly delivered in order to vindicate the death of their loved one.

Often victims' families feel they are caught in a macabre game where the prosecution and police are arrayed on one side against the defense teams on the other side, both teams vying for the upper hand, with justice and right falling by the wayside.

Each part of the process seemed to take an inordinately long time, but maybe that was because we didn't understand the whole process. Fortunately for us, the prosecution dedicated themselves to fairness and expediency in Steve's case.

The police enlisted volunteers from a metal detector club to carefully scan the open field near the location of the taxi where Steve's body was discovered. They spent hours carefully tracing the ground, hoping to recover bullets that had pierced the windshield after passing through Steve's head. They found nothing.

Then the detectives learned that the previous owner of the gun the suspect was believed to have purchased had conducted random target practice in his back yard. The detective requested permission to search the yard for spent bullets. He found several at the site, enough to conduct ballistic tests with the fragment of a bullet found in the cab. The resulting evidence was strong enough to lodge a murder charge against the suspect.

I was amazed at the tenacity of the police. In their periodic reports to us about the investigation, they rarely seemed discouraged. Perhaps they were merely trying to keep our spirits optimistic. But in every call we received from them, they spoke reassuringly about the progress of their investigation.

Only as time passed did we realize how unrelenting the detectives were in pursuing Steve's murderer. They spent hours and hours in painstaking search for the smallest clues. They followed each little lead with dogged persistence. Even after the suspect was in custody, the careful search for evidence continued.

They reported objectively on each progression in their search for clues. Because of their imperturbable attitude, I continued to have hope that the killer would be convicted before he could harm someone else.

THE FACE OF A MURDERER

Finally, in January, the gathered evidence was presented to the grand jury, which returned an indictment of first-degree murder. Grand juries are closed to spectators and press alike, so we knew only the final outcome of the proceedings.

The police continued to search for further clues. Voice samples of the suspect were finally obtained and sent for analysis. Police interviewed numerous people who might have some idea of what had taken place.

Jerry and I were traveling during the initial public court hearings, but we hurried home to join our daughters in the courtroom the second day of the hearings.

I felt surprisingly neutral at my first view of the accused murderer. Although I had seen his picture in the newspaper, seeing him in person didn't elicit the strong feelings of rage or despair or grief I had anticipated. Instead, I felt a huge wave of loss sweep over me. How could this man take Steve from us? How could he deliberately blow away his head, watch him die, and then walk away? Such cruelty was incomprehensible to me. Standing in shackles in the courtroom, he didn't seem particularly threatening, although some of his behavior appeared bizarre to me.

Further psychiatric examinations were ordered by court-appointed and defense-selected psychiatrists. Another date was set for the presentation of those findings. The accused murderer was found competent to stand trial.

In a subsequent hearing, the accused murderer stated he wanted to dismiss his attorneys and confess to the crime of second-degree murder. In exchange for providing the weapon, which police had been unable to find, he would plead guilty to second-degree murder and receive the mandatory sentencing of forty-eight years in prison.

He stated that he wanted to be sentenced and begin serving his time. His defense attorneys objected, but the judge, after considerable examination of precedents, allowed the confession.

Jerry and I, weeping silently, sat in the courtroom along with Julie and our daughters. We were surrounded by friends and other family members as we heard the confessed killer say, "I shot Steve White three times in the back of the head." He offered no explanation or excuse for Steve's murder.

The sitting judge accepted his confession and sentenced him to a total of fifty-six years in prison. Without emotion or demonstration, the murderer received the sentence and was led away. Throughout the entire proceeding, I felt a tragic affair was coming to a close. A fitting conclusion to a brutal action. There would be some justice for Steve's senseless death.

Yet the young man who killed Steve still had life, while Steve's life was over. Without explanation of the killer's actions, we still knew no *reason* for Steve's death. That is what most families of homicide victims face. Even when the murderer gives some explanation, there simply is never a reason to justify killing another human being.

Following that court hearing, we were interviewed

ʒain by television and newspaper reporters. At last we left the courthouse, and as a group we went to the cemetery to sit around Steve's grave, talk together of the past year, pray together, and feel some sense of comfort that in the months since Steve's death we had found healing and justice was served.

GONE BUT NOT FORGOTTEN

It was a lovely spring day, unlike the blustery weather on his burial day a year before. We sat in the freshly mown grass, enjoying the scents and sounds of springtime. As I listened to the elation in the conversation around me, and heard the laughter of my loved ones, I relished the healing that had come in the year since Steve's terrible murder. We had been drawn into the most horrifying of losses, but we had survived to live and laugh again.

I thought back to the previous year when Jerry and I were traveling much of the last month of Steve's life. Several times I called him during the early morning hours while he was working at the radio station. I will always be grateful for those conversations, a memory that lasts even now.

Steve's murder left such a gaping hole in my life. I had watched the passage of his life for thirty years, and abruptly that was cut off. I would never see him achieve his goals, never watch him reach middle age, never again enjoy those spontaneous visits, gifts, and talks that had become so much a part of our relationship. I would desperately miss all of the special touches my relationship with Steve held.

If we ever called to ask a favor, he was quick to respond—a ride to the airport, help moving furniture, assistance in the garden. One time I needed minor surgery that required a brief hospital stay of a few hours. Because Jerry was traveling, Steve came to the hospital, stayed with me, drove me home, and cared for me until I felt well enough to stay alone.

Steve made a habit of stopping by our house, taking time to drink a Coke and talk for a while. I grew to anticipate his yellow cab pulling into the driveway. I thoroughly enjoyed those spontaneous visits. We discussed his work, gardening, local politics, international affairs, family events. Occasionally he told me of humorous or touching or threatening incidents in his taxi. Although I urged caution, Steve assured me he knew the situations to avoid.

If I wasn't at home, he would often leave a little note, a quickly composed poem, a wildflower, some produce from his garden, some small memento of his visit. On his last impromptu visit to our house, he didn't find me at home. He quickly composed a little poem on a scrap of paper and left it on the kitchen counter. The upbeat message comforted me after his death. It seemed almost prophetic in its message.

Hey, hey, hey,
How's your day?
Just dropped by on the way
To say things are A-OK!

Love, Stephen

When we returned home after learning of his murder, there was a brief message from him on our answering machine.

"Hi, how's everybody? Just calling to see how you are, but guess you aren't home right now. I'll talk to you later. See you later."

How difficult, how painful to hear Steve's voice and know I'd never hear it again on this earth. But, Steve, dear Steve, I will talk to you later. And yes, I will see you later.

And then we faced Steve's first death day. Before Steve's murder, I didn't even know such an expression existed. How powerful a description of our sorrow. Steve had a *birth* day, now he had a *death* day.

Jerry and I spent that day in quiet and solitude, taking a brief vacation. I didn't want the day to pass. I feared a fading of the memories of Steve's life. I feared that with the passing of all the *firsts* in that first year of loss, Steve's life and death would be minimized and forgotten.

Then a florist van drove to the door delivering several bouquets, letting us know that Steve had not been forgotten. Friends were still reaching out in comfort and love. The mail carrier, too, brought a packet of letters and cards, tangible evidence that others were remembering Steve and thinking of us.

I wanted a special sign that day, a message that all of the pain, the sleepless nights, the endless tears, the deep grief in missing Steve had been worth it. And as I sat in quiet contemplation on the beach in Florida, two verses I had learned in childhood drifted through my mind.

Precious in the sight of the Lord is the death of his saints (Psalm 115:16).

My comfort in my suffering is this. Your promise preserves my life (Psalm 119:50).

A message for Steve. A word for me. God knew it all—Steve's eternal joy, my sorrow. And He would *bring it all together for good because we love Him.*

Chapter 14

LIVING WITH GRIEF

Spiritual refreshment brings completion to the grief process. Although my heart was bruised and broken, I felt a strong bond with God, stronger than at any time before in my life. With everything adrift around me—my equilibrium shattered—only God remained a stable element, an immovable force in my life.

We had been told that the fourth to seventh months following a loved one's death are the most difficult, because that is when it finally becomes real that your loved one is gone. The sharp pain I first experienced following Steve's death lessened enough to allow a flood of thoughts of the future that loomed bleak and hostile.

Ironically, most grieving people initially focus on the *future*, imagining the difficult life ahead without their loved one. The years stretch empty and painful and lonely. Only as we begin to remember the past with joy and warmth and gratitude do we realize we are beginning to heal.

Heaven became a reality to me during that time. I let my imagination wander freely, speculating on the atmosphere, the pleasures of Heaven. I imagined Steve there, picturing what he might be doing. I thought often of other relatives who had died—our parents, grandparents, aunts and uncles. I felt comforted as I thought of Steve welcomed by them. He was especially close to his great-grandmother. She had died just a scant nine months before he did.

Steve, dear, did you see Grandma? I'm sure she welcomed you with all of the love she showed you here, and more. It helps me so much to know you are with so many who loved you here, and now love you there.

Reading the psalms helped me immensely. The writers of the ancient psalms understood sorrow, trouble, loss, and tragedy. I felt a kinship and encouragement as I repeatedly read those inspired words. I took heart from those poetic writings that expressed such an understanding of human sorrow. They reveal God's love and comfort available to everyone who grieves.

A little verse I had kept on my desk for years seemed to agree with the helpful words in the psalms.

Sometimes the Lord calms the storm.
Sometimes He lets the storm rage
    and calms His child.

The storm raged all around me, but deep in my inner core there was calm. Steve was safe and loved. God had welcomed him to Heaven. God had not abandoned me here.

I will never leave you nor forsake you. I am with you always (Joshua 1:5, Matthew 28:20).

I spent a lot of time reading the psalms in several translations and paraphrases. Passages that I had known from childhood took on new meaning as I saw them in the light of my own suffering.

I weep with grief. My heart is heavy with sorrow;
*   encourage and cheer me with your words.*
*   (Psalm 119:28)*

My comfort in my suffering is this: Your promise
*   preserves my life. (Psalm 119:50)*

Though you have made me see troubles, many
*   and bitter, you will restore my life again; and*
*   comfort me once again. (Psalm 71:20)*

139

I thought often of the words of Jesus.

> *"Blessed are those who mourn, for they will be comforted." (Matthew 5:4)*

And then a lovely verse impressed me as I read Psalms.

> *"Blessed are the people whose God is the LORD." (Psalm 144:15)*

Dear God, You alone are enough for me when I am suffering this deeply. As I rest in the comfort of Your love, I will find solace in my mourning.

God was the one unchanging stability in my emotionally tilting universe. He knew my mourning; He knew just how severe my suffering was. He offered comfort and rest for my battered soul. In time, with His gentle help, healing came.

He would bring some good from all of the pain, all of the terrible sorrow. In my early grief I couldn't imagine that good would ever come again, but slowly, slowly, life again brought joy.

I will never again be as carefree and lighthearted as I was in the past. I have known deep grief, as well as its attending comfort and healing. I have been sobered. I recognize the fragility of life, the valuable gift of relationships. I have known unbearable sorrow, and I've survived only because of the love of God and dear friends. Through the pain I can hope to share comfort with others who walk the same sad path of grief.

> *Lord, if like a fragile flower*
> *Torn petal by petal*
> *My heart must continue to tear,*
> *Let there be fragrance.*

Psalm 23, which Fred whispered to me that desolate burial day in the cemetery, came to encourage me again and again.

He restores my soul.

Truly, my soul and Jerry's were broken. But only the broken things of life need *restoration*, and that is what God offered us as we kept looking to Him for healing.

He will comfort all who mourn, and provide for those who grieve . . . , to bestow on them a crown of beauty instead of ashes, the oil of gladness instead of mourning, and a garment of praise instead of a spirit of despair (Isaiah 61:2-3).

AFTERWORD

by
Jerry
White

My grandson Jerad was riding with his mother in their car. He was uncharacteristically quiet for an exuberant three-year-old. Suddenly he asked Karen, "Can Steve come to our house to play?" She replied, "No, dear, he can't. Steve is in Heaven."

"You mean he can never come to my house again?"

"No, honey, never."

There was a long pause. Finally Jerad plaintively said, "But I want him to."

And so do Mary and I. But it will never be. No amount of desire, longing, or regret can turn back the clock and reverse the tragic footprint of history. A thousand "what ifs" have flown through our minds as we so desperately wish we would have done something to get Steve out of his taxi-driving job. But all the wishes in the world will not bring him back. We live in the present reality, and we learn to cope. And we even learn to experience true happiness again.

Mary has chronicled the events of that first year so indelibly stamped in our minds. She has shared the sorrow and the first glimpses of joy. I deeply share her feelings. They truly reflect our stumbling journey.

Today the sharp pain of early grief has lessened. Time does deaden human feelings. But the vacuum in our lives remains. We know where Steve is today; that gives us incredible comfort. We go on with purpose, experiencing the blessing of our three daughters and our eight grandchildren. They, too, have been affected by these events in ways that even we do not fully comprehend.

Today the story goes on. The man who confessed to Steve's murder is now appealing his confession on the basis of insanity. He also confessed to a shooting in a Florida convenience store, thinking he had killed the man. In reality, he shot his arm off. At this writing, he is standing trial in Florida, again pleading insanity. We are not angry, bitter, or vindictive toward him. We do want justice to be done and the public protected.

Kristie greatly missed Steve at her July 1994 wedding. There was an unspoken void without him. Other family events continue to be reminders of the broken family bonds.

On my personal journey in the first months following Steve's murder, I found myself not caring about much of anything except getting through the next day. As challenging and exciting as my task of leading the worldwide Navigators organization is, I found that it faded into the background, crushed by the weight of grief. Any thoughts of ego or pride stemming from my position became virtually inconsequential. I had to rebuild my thinking, my motivation—and to some degree, my beliefs (theology). But the process was good. The wounds of my life gave others the chance to help me and to see more of my inner life and my weaknesses.

Mary has expressed the cry of her heart, and it is the cry of mine too. I still find it difficult to see how we lived through those first days and weeks. In some ways they are a blur. In other ways, the horror and sorrow stand out in bold, clear memory.

Personally, I have wrestled with regret as much as sorrow. I recall the times when I was too busy to play with Steve, when I could have been with him more, when discipline and harsh words were spoken as he bore the brunt of the expectations of a firstborn son, when I could have listened more and understood more of his inner thoughts and longings.

My battle with regret led me to a deeper under-standing of myself, my weaknesses, and the imperfec-tion of being a human father. I had to realize that in my inexperience and youth, I did the best I could as a father. But even that understanding only took a small edge off the pain. This entire journey has given new meaning to friendships and relationships. And it has caused me to refocus my life in many ways.

Through it all, I have learned that life is frail, tem-porary. It is valuable and meaningful. It is filled with joys and sorrows. It is dependent on others for its completeness. It carries wounds that are miraculously healed. It is fragile yet resilient. But, above all, life is eternal in its spirit. There is more to life than just being alive. There is an eternal life with God that supersedes all the goals of humanity.

As a father, I have traveled a path I would wish on no one. Yet it is a path that leads to a deeper life, one that resonates with love, not anger. I am puzzled that we have not been more angry. In some ways I cannot help but think of Steve's murderer as the son of sor-rowing parents. Their hopes also have been dashed. And he also is a human being in desperate need of God's love and forgiveness.

In this book, Mary has revealed some of the deep-est thoughts of her heart in the hope that they will touch the hidden feelings of other parents who have encountered shattered dreams through the death of their children. Our hope and prayer is that others will find comfort in knowing they are not alone—that friends, and most especially God Himself, care about the heartache they feel.

Appendix A

A ROAD MAP
THROUGH GRIEF

Every grief journey is an untraveled road. Even those who have suffered severe grief earlier in life experience fresh sorrow with each new loss. Every loving relationship has its own special dynamics. When that person is gone, the pain of the loss washes over the soul with terrible intensity.

Although no one can assign a grieving process to another, there are similarities in each grief experience. Knowing what to expect in general helps one to anticipate the journey. This knowledge doesn't make the process easier, but it does verify some common ground with other grieving people. It confirms that the grieving person isn't crazy or weak, or even obstinately clinging to grief for too long a time.

We can't practice for grief; we can't take lessons to prepare for it. Loss comes and we're suddenly, unwillingly underway in a sorrowful pilgrimage. All of our life experiences, and our relationship with the loved one, will determine how we grieve.

There is no right or wrong way to grieve. Diverse cultures, indeed, varied personalities, express grief differently. Some are open and vocal and outwardly emotional about their grief. Others are reserved, stoic, quiet. Is one right and the other wrong? Certainly not. The depth of grief cannot be assessed by the style of expression.

Grief arrives in one of two ways. There is *sudden loss* through accidents, suicide, heart attacks, strokes, homicide. And there is *anticipated loss* through illness and aging. Anticipated loss allows for some preparation and a loving farewell, but it brings increased sorrow while watching the beloved one suffer. All loss brings wrenching pain as our loved ones are torn from us.

Grief comes like the waves of the sea. Several small waves wash over us, and then without warning, triggered perhaps by a memory of the loved one, a huge wave of anguish smashes on the shores of our souls and knocks us down. As we pick ourselves up and go on, the waves keep coming. Eventually, the enormous swells of pain diminish to a bearable degree.

The waves allow two steps forward before pulling us one step back. But always, slowly, forward movement comes.

Here are several suggestions that may help you on the grief journey.

PACE YOURSELF

Grief is the hardest work you will ever do. It drains you of physical, emotional, and spiritual stamina. Unless you pace yourself and direct your energies toward grief recovery, you can experience physical illness, emotional despair, relational detachments, and spiritual bitterness. Even when you do pace your grief, those negative elements may intrude. You must allow time to process the grief and recover.

LEAN INTO THE PAIN

Face the grief head-on. It's tempting to plunge into a hectic round of activity to avoid facing the grief, but it's useless to do so. The grief will be there waiting long after the pace has slowed. The more quickly you confront the loss, the more quickly healthy recovery will begin.

GET READY FOR A SECOND WAVE OF GRIEF

The period of four to seven months following the death is often the most difficult. Reality sets in. Shock wears off. At that point grieving people grasp the enormity of their loss. They recognize the cruel truth that life will never be the same.

It is also about this time that friends think grievers should be feeling "normal" again. This feeling may result in diminished sympathy, tolerance, and help for your continued mourning. During this period you need to be gentle with yourself, guarding your physical health, giving way to emotional pain, and seeking spiritual stimulus and help.

TRUST THE RECOVERY PROCESS

It takes nearly two years following a death loss to gain equilibrium and stabilization in physical and emotional health. The time frame may run as high as three years following a homicide or suicide.

Our society doesn't allow for this healing period. We live at a fast pace and are expected to resume normal life, normal responses, normal reactions in a short period of time. It doesn't happen that way. You may sustain your work schedule, but most likely your effectiveness will be reduced and your emotions put on hold while you struggle to recover.

WELCOME HELP FROM THOSE WHO LOVE YOU

People who love you will want to help. Accept that help with gratitude. Receiving the aid of loving friends and family is a step toward healing. It gives the reassurance that you are not alone, that there are others on whom you can lean. Don't be hesitant to ask friends for help as you move through the maze of complicated emotions and detailed decisions.

PROTECT YOUR PHYSICAL HEALTH

Guarding physical health involves simple measures— balanced nutrition, light exercise, and rest. Although these are common and elementary steps to good health, they can be extraordinarily difficult during a grief period. You either don't want to eat, or you eat far too much of the wrong thing. You feel you have no energy to exercise. All of your energies are directed toward grieving.

You resist trying to rest, because during periods of inactivity your mind focuses relentlessly on your loss. If you can discipline yourself to protect your health, you will find more energy to deal with your loss and less illness to distract you.

REFUSE TO LIVE WITH REGRETS

Some grieving people are tempted to batter themselves emotionally for past mistakes or omissions with the loved one who is gone. Even if regrets are valid, they cannot change the facts. You have to forgive yourself and forgive the one who died, and make a strong effort to come to terms with the finality of the death.

AVOID MAJOR CHANGES

Delay making major decisions and life changes immediately following the death of a loved one. Rational thinking and careful judgment desert you at this time. Even wise counsel from loving friends may prove wrong as they cannot fully know the best course. Unless forced by finances or legal pressures, wait to make significant decisions.

LOOK BEYOND PEOPLE'S WORDS

Be willing to tolerate people who are less than helpful. People will say and do things that they hope will help, but instead may only increase the grief. Look beyond the stereotyped phrases to the intent of the person.

Occasionally, a truly distorted person will say things calculated to discover the depth of suffering, and even try to intensify it. Avoid those people. Grieving people need caring, not curious or cruel, people surrounding them as they recover.

LET YOUR GRIEF BENEFIT OTHERS

With small steps, begin to reach out to others, for in giving help and care to someone else, your own wounded soul is restored. When we extend ourselves to others, even in small ways, we share another's burden while finding rest for our souls.

Appendix B

A NATION UNDER SIEGE

Most people have contact with murder only through television or movies or books. Homicide is neutralized in these settings. The victims either have no personality or are so gruesomely unreal that their deaths mean nothing. They are simply an expendable part of the storyline. These fictitious presentations of murder discredit and diminish the genuine suffering that results from the wave of homicides occurring every day in this country.

The murdered loved one is referred to as the *victim*. But for every homicide victim there are dozens, often hundreds, of secondary victims—family and friends who reel under the blow of losing their precious loved one in such a pointless and brutal way.

The toll murder takes in the United States is enormous. We have, by far, the highest murder rate in the world. Steve died in 1990. That year 24,932 people were murdered in the U.S. When I think of the suffering and anguish we, as Steve's family and friends, felt in the wake of his murder, and multiply it by nearly 25,000, the magnitude of sorrow is incalculable. And the statistics keep climbing every year.

Beyond the personal grief of those left behind, this nation bears a tremendous loss: The victims' potential contribution to our society—their skills, talents, and abilities—is forever cut off. An immense and tragic loss.

Many, many murders are never solved, leaving families and friends in limbo and pain. To further compound the loss, many confessed and convicted murderers receive ridiculously light sentences for their crimes. They are often paroled early only to kill again.

These vicious killers place themselves above the law of the land and far outside the laws of God. By some perverted twist of thinking, these self-appointed assassins assume the right to kill whenever and whomever they choose. They step into the shoes of God, deciding when and how another human being will die.

They murder in rage, they murder for personal gain, they murder to demonstrate power, they murder on a whim, they murder in cruelty. They murder babies, children, the innocent, the helpless, and sometimes they murder their enemies.

They use weapons of all descriptions—cars, clubs, knives—even their own hands and brute strength. By far, they use firearms as the weapon of choice. It is the weapon of a coward, for it almost certainly seals the doom of the victim. Human flesh has no protection against a penetrating rain of steel bullets.

We are the only civilized country in the world that has allowed unrestricted use of handguns. Slowly that is changing. We can endlessly argue the intent of the authors of our Constitution when they wrote the second amendment. Should the militia have the right to keep and bear arms? Just who is the militia? Does that mean the common citizen today? Should there be no restriction for the insane, the criminal, the underage?

In Steve's case, the confessed murderer, a known felon, purchased the handgun in a pawn shop six days before he blew away the back of Steve's head. He used his given name. No check was made into his background, his criminal record. He simply paid for the gun, walked out of the shop with it in hand, and murdered Steve.

Some would say that our experience is an exception, that rarely does a criminal purchase a gun using his given name. How many *exceptions* should society tolerate?

Should the parents, siblings, spouse of a murder victim care if someone wanting to target practice with a pistol gets hostile because he has to wait a few days to purchase one? I think not. Gun management and regulation, not *control*, simply makes sense.

In discussing some type of gun regulation with Julie, she said she had read that a gun collector considered any gun regulation an "inconvenience."

She was understandably outraged when she heard that, and she told me, "It was quite an *inconvenience* to lose my husband."

Certainly, law-abiding and sane citizens of legal age have every right to purchase, maintain, and own firearms. But what about the insane, the convicted criminal, the underage? Should we do nothing to prevent lethal weapons from falling into their hands?

A year after Steve's death, Jerry and I were asked to appear before a congressional committee considering the pros and cons of the Brady bill. We joined several other parents and spouses who went to Capitol Hill to tell of their suffering following the senseless murder of their loved ones.

One father tried to tell of the shooting death of his youngest son, a Yale University student, the month before. His son had been walking near the campus. A young man approached him, pulled a gun from his pocket, and gunned him down without provocation or explanation.

The despairing father couldn't finish his prepared statement. His daughter, her head leaning on her father's shoulder, finished the story in a shaking voice.

In our testimony, Jerry and I tried to emphasize the injustice of Steve's death, the terrible waste of his life. If provisions to restrict criminals from purchasing guns had been in place and operative, Steve's murderer would never have been allowed to purchase a handgun. I found it terribly difficult in that solemn public forum to recount the details of Steve's senseless death, and my voice broke a number of times.

The tangible sorrow of the victims' families permeated that solemn chamber as parents told of their children dying, and a young widow told of her husband's murder. We represented only a small number of the suffering families in the United States.

I have yet to meet a loved one of a murder victim, no matter how conservative politically in other arenas, who does not strongly support reasonable restrictions to reduce the murder rate in this country. This would include much stiffer penalties for violent crime, less leniency from parole boards, limited gun regulation, and many other efforts to reduce the tragic loss of life in our society.

The police in this country fight overwhelming odds against a swelling wave of increasingly vicious lawlessness. They see their fellow officers cruelly murdered and wonder if they will be next. When will a simple traffic stop result in a rain of bullets and death? When will an enraged lunatic cut loose with an assault weapon merely for hatred of the police? These men and women show more courage each day than most of us demonstrate in a lifetime.

Although nothing can take away our pain and loneliness in the wake of Steve's unjust death, there is a certain comfort in sharing with those who have suffered the same loss and reviewing the convoluted attitude toward crime that allowed it to happen.

From the beginning of our ordeal I knew that ultimate justice would rest with God. But I have now watched our justice system in action. If, in some small way, we can make it more efficient in curbing crime and the terrible sorrow that results, we want to be a part.